PER

PEACE

On Your Way to

GREATNESS

*A Guide into Mind
and Spiritual Awakening*

CHRISTOPHER FORD

outskirts
press

Table of Contents

Introduction

Life can be inexplicably great, especially knowing that the Lord will never give you more than you can bear! This world is dark for the ones who do not know how to access Christ's almighty power. God's favor is upon all of us. God may use people for different situations. But we all have a purpose in this life. What is yours?

Faith in Jesus will make your dreams come true. Trust all that you have comes from Him. Your family, home, finances, health, and most importantly, your mind. The reason why this book is called *"**Perfect Peace**"* is because that is where your heart belongs. Jesus says, "That He will give you peace beyond your understanding." After reading this book, it will show you how real the anointing and "Perfect Peace" is in Christ. Jesus is not a myth or a fairy tale. It is an historical fact that Jesus walked upon the Earth. Multitudes of people saw Him.

If every miracle that Jesus had performed were documented, His miracles would fill every book in all of the libraries, on the whole entire Earth. His power is omnipotent and unfailing. Jesus existed before the beginning of time. I Am, an oneness, which is always present, an oneness that resides inside of you and all living things. Jesus is a part of the Holy Trinity: the Father, the Son, and the Holy Ghost that forms into one spirit.

Christ's coming had been prophesied for many thousands of years before He even stepped foot upon the Earth. Many religions around the world mirrored the prophesy of Christ and adopted it as their own. Those other religions just placed their own god in His place because there was nothing before Christ, the Holy Trinity.

It is the devil's job to establish doubt and lies about Christ. The devil knew Christ was coming to the Earth to save the wretched. The devil has been upon the Earth long before humans were created. Jesus already warned His believers about false prophets coming. Jesus said people will be on the Earth saying "There He is" or "Here He is!"

Jesus knew that He would be rejected by this generation. If Jesus and the Bible is not real, how did Jesus and the Bible state with precision what will happen upon the Earth 2,000 years later? Jesus's crucifixion was prophesied in the Old Testament a thousand years before He was born.

Multitudes of people were waiting for His coming because they understood that Christ had not yet come to the Earth. Everything happened exactly like the prophets had said a thousand years earlier. In the times of those prophecies, crucifixion was not even a method of execution. Crucifixion was not a form of execution in that region until around 71 BC. Therefore, the prophets in the Bible prophesied the crucifixion approximately 929 years before it was even practiced in the area.

The crucifixion has been documented in history by many credible individuals during that time. For example, highly qualified ancient historians such as Thallus and Phlegon recorded the absolutely rare event in 33 B.C. of the sun going dark for three hours! The moon can only cover the sun during an eclipse for less than eight minutes. Only God can control the movements of the celestial bodies. He uses them as signs.

"For God so loved the world that He gave His only begotten son, and whosoever believed in Him should not perish, but will have everlasting life." Religion should not divide humanity at all. All religions should be respected. Religion should not tell you to kill people for their disbelief. That is just insane. Your lord or god should be able to handle that on his own.

Religion is not a competition. No religion should tell you to kill anyone. Instead, it should tell you to love one another. With Christ you are not on a prayer schedule. As Christians, all day is prayer time because Christians pray without ceasing. With Christ you can speak to situations in life, and the situations will obey you. With Christ you are already healed from any ailment or disease. In Christ you are already more than a conqueror.

"Lean not to thy own understanding." But through Christ the truth will be made known. If you search for the knowledge of Christ, you will surely find it. Jesus was God's lamb. He was sacrificed for all men and women. After Jesus was sacrificed and rose from the dead, all other sacrifices were to cease. Animal sacrifices could only merely cover sin. But the sacrifice of Jesus wiped all sin away so that humanity may live with Him eternally.

He settled everything on the cross. Jesus Christ is the greatest gift of all! He is Christmas every day. He is alive with all power in His hands. Jesus, the savior, was not made up by anyone. That is the biggest lie ever told in the Universe. People who say that have not done any extensive research at all. They are just spreading vicious lies, which is utterly contrary to history and the Word.

There are some instances when history has to rewrite itself completely. For example, "The Lemba Clan" in Ethiopia are the descendants from the long-lost tribe of Jerusalem. The very same long-lost Black Jews from Israel, which was said to have never existed. In Axum Ethiopia, there are relics from Moses and Jesus himself! Jesus, Mary, and Joseph lived in Axum for three months and six days. Menelik I, Solomon's son, brought the Ark of the Covenant to Ethiopia around 950 B.C.

Just recently, a petroglyph was found in Israel in some ancient ruins. The petroglyph was inscribed with Goliath's name on it. It was dated to the exact time period the Bible said Goliath existed. That evidence confirmed the David and Goliath story. It really happened after all. History said that the David and Goliath story was only a myth. The historians also said that the Old Testament was heavily fabricated to exaggerate David's greatness.

History or science will never catch up to the Word of God. Science is just a story in itself and will continue to evolve. Not too long ago, the

Earth was considered flat by scientists. There is a planet beyond Pluto in the Earth's solar system. Scientists and astronomers said in the past that this planet did not exist. Recently, with their high-tech telescopes, this planet was discovered.

Ancient cultures of old already knew of this planet. The Sumerians mapped this planet on a rock tablet thousands of years ago. The Mayans charted this planet in their pyramid structures. Those pyramid structures were spaced out with the exact mathematical distances of the planets in between them. There is much information to learn from and about other cultures.

Search extensively for knowledge because some knowledge is hidden. No one knows everything, and mistakes will be made on the way. Is it really a mistake if you learn a valuable lesson from it? It is absolutely necessary to stand on the shoulders of past thinkers, evangelists, prophets, prophetesses, philosophers, historians, astronomers, scientists, and various cultures.

Do not just leave it up to the historians and scientists to get everything right. This is another example why: Ancient Rivers that have been mentioned in Genesis were discredited by archeologists and historians also. History said that the ancient rivers in Genesis never existed until recently with the invention of Google Earth. Those ancient rivers have been discovered. These ancient rivers have been discovered exactly where the Bible placed them. The Pishon River is one of them, for example. Even the Sumerians and ancient Egyptians did not know about the Pishon. But the Word of God did.

The ancient Sumerians and Egyptians are considered to be the first beginning of our known civilization. But the Bible mentions rivers with exact precision many thousands of years before their existence. Maybe the Bible needs to be taken literally at its word? Furthermore, history and science still have a long way to go. It was said before that these people, relics, planets, or rivers never existed. They were only recognized as myths or fairy tales until recently....

Jesus said, "Knowledge will be increased at the end of time." That is why your own research is vital. Do not take other people's word for it. A person that is seeking God should not just go to church and let the preacher do all of the spiritual work. There is a right and wrong way to divide the "Word of Truth". Not every preacher has been taught the right way to explain the Word of Truth, resulting in people having a wrong interpretation about Jesus.

The Bible is not here to make the reader feel bad about themselves. The Bible is here to show the reader ultimately how perfect they are in Christ Jesus. The search for truth and knowledge on your own is extremely liberating. There is much to learn about Jesus every single day. One day a week is not enough time with Him. A relationship must be built with Jesus so that trust in Him can be impregnable.

The devil is working through nonbelievers as his vessel to spread disbelief to weak-minded people around the Earth. Those nonbelievers are Satan's loud speaker. They are lost sheep that have been led astray and are on their way to get devoured. Lost minds think that Christianity shackles the mind. Truthfully, Christianity only transforms and liberates the mind. It transforms the mind to heal the sick and to raise the dead.

One of the worst things people can do to themselves is to think that they are free when they are really enslaved. Without God, a person is surely lost and totally enslaved. Jesus opened up the prison doors. So without Him, it is like sitting in prison for life with all of the doors wide open. Suffering while thinking you are enjoying is an illusion.

Faith in what really works has been diminished by nonbelievers. For example, nonbelievers have been going around saying that healing does not exist. They would say or ask, "Jesus was made up by a white man" or "why does Horus and others have the same story as Jesus?" "But what about the Egyptians?" All of those stories were echoing the tradition of Christ's coming. Christ's blood sacrifice for the world was ordained to come since the beginning of time. He is the Alpha and Omega. He is the "Word". The Word became a "Man" and made His dwelling amongst us. Jesus is the finished work. When He died on the cross for humanity, all of the other myths, sacrifices, and prophesies were put to rest after the cross. It was finished! *Finito*!

Those stories are still relevant to history. But Jesus died for the whole world. All of the sins and judgments upon Christ's sheep was drawn unto Him. Do not follow man. Follow the Holy Spirit. Man used to worship the sun. Egyptians used to worship statues, dogs, stars, and golden cows. History shows you that humans are followers of anything moving or inanimate. Whatever someone else is doing in society that is trendy, weak-minded people will follow it. They will follow everything except the Truth and the Light. This process is called operating in spiritual blindness. A blind person cannot see light.

There are an inestimable amount of suns/stars in the universe, but the lack of knowledge made people follow others to worship the sun. Lack of knowledge will cause people to do all manner of ludicrous things. Get consciousness through your own extensive search for knowledge. The people in this material world know not what they are saying or doing. The only reason why the Earth is even still here is because of the Lord.

Never degrade anyone's religion. Let them continue to seek so they will find the light. Christ will find His way into their hearts, too. There is no other love like His, nor will there ever be! His love is sweeter than honey dew. With just only one taste of Jesus Christ's love and peace, it will have an everlasting effect that will never fade away or diminish.

Use the word "consciousness" for a way to be aware. Use consciousness for the way it is really meant to be used. Never be at war with yourself on your way to full consciousness. You will have to first know who and whose you are. That is the only way to gain any type of full consciousness.

God gave us all free will. Why not give your people free will? North Korea and other oppressive countries--what are you afraid of? Are you afraid of people realizing who they really are in Christ? Do not worry. All of that will be made plain and clear very soon. Let us love each other while we are here on this Earth. If anything, religion should band us together. We are all looking to a higher power to make us great. Let us be great together.

Let us stop the cycle of hate because hate is a very powerful force and energy. Your hate energy can be felt by other people and animals. Hate only perpetuates hate. Let us perpetuate love and giving. It does not make you weak. In fact, it makes you very strong in the mind. You can only win through your display of love. Spread love, and more love will be spread unto you.

What if you want to flex and show off your ego? For example, fighting, arguing, and killing one another? That road will only lead to disaster or strife for yourself and future generations. Your future family, children, and environment will be impacted. Let us make a shift in consciousness as a whole. Let us do it together.

Focusing and meditating on the Word will create in you a better person. Your life and energy impacts others on this beautiful planet. We are all interconnected. You cannot see the energy, but you can feel it. Just as you cannot see the air, but you breathe it. For instance, it is just like having a room in a house. The space in the room is the most important because without the space, it would not even be a room. Space makes up 99% of the Universe. The space is invisible, but is most important. So it is the unseen that is the most important in life.

Take control of your mind. It starts with you. One person at a time. Do not wait until someone else makes a move. Be the example. Be the one that creates the invention to change the whole world. Let it be seen in you the way to live. Smile big! Laugh-because you know who you are and exactly where you are going. Your positive energy will be felt around the globe. It starts with you. Right now...

Chapter One

Perfect Peace

On Your Way to Greatness

Greatness

Greatness is allowing God to build through you a life and a legacy that not only impacts you, but other generations as well for His glory. *__Genesis 12:1-3...__* Your greatness must be for the glory of God. Reaching for greatness should be an everyday ritual.

Envisioning your goals and dreams every day is necessary. A vision is a portrait of possibility for your life. Just being good at what you do is okay, but you should be shooting and reaching for greatness. Just being good gets in the way of greatness. Good is just a crutch not to be great. And if greatness is truly in you? Which it is... It will eventually come out wherever you are. It does not matter where you come from or the pigment of your skin.

God turned Joseph's life around into greatness. He was thrown into a cistern or a pit by his jealous brothers. Then, his brothers sold him into slavery for twenty shekels of silver to the Ishmaelite's. *__Genesis 37:23...__* The Ishmaelite's later sold Joseph to Potiphar, the chief of Pharaoh's guards. Potiphar started to recognize that God was with Joseph in all that he did. The Lord granted Joseph success in everything. Potiphar eventually placed Joseph in charge of all of the possessions that he owned. The situation was going well until Potiphar's wife started to have lustful eyes for Joseph. Joseph was well-built and very handsome.

One day Potiphar's wife lied and accused Joseph of trying to sleep with her. So Potiphar grew angry and threw Joseph into prison. *__Genesis 39:11-18...__* But even in prison, Joseph's greatness shone through like the star Betelgeuse! God was with Joseph in everything that he did.

Joseph had a wonderful gift in interpreting dreams. The Pharaoh of Egypt had some dreams that no one else but Joseph could inter-pret. After Joseph interpreted the Pharaoh's dreams with precision, the Pharaoh was astonished and released him from prison, and then placed Joseph in charge of the whole land of Egypt. ***Genesis 41:39-43...*** God turned what looked like total disaster into total greatness because Joseph trusted totally in Him.

You have been picked for your situation. You may even feel that you are not qualified for the vision God has given you. The vision may just be too big! But trust God because God chose you for that big vision. You may not be qualified, but you are chosen. Be great! ***Gen. 39:2...*** It is essential to have courage and believe in yourself. Think great things about yourself because as long as God puts breathe into your body, you can make a great breakthrough. Your actions every day should be marching toward greatness.

You can only be great if you think that you are. Think and eat great-ness. Smell the breath of greatness. Ninety-eight percent of people are spending 98% of their time on insignificant things. They are spend-ing precious time on things that have nothing to do with their purpose or greatness in life.

It is pointless to do insignificant or bad things. Only do things that add substance to your life. Ask Obama, can he be the first Black President of the United States of America? We must have the audacity to hope. We must have the audacity to see things that are not there yet. Call out things which be not as though they were. ***Romans 4:17...***

Do not dare think that there will not be any opposition or obstacles on your way because humanity is at war. Not against flesh and blood, but against wickedness in high places. ***Ephesians 6:12...*** This means that there are many demons that do not want to see you be great. They want to suppress who you really are in Christ. No one can truly be great without the one and only, "I AM" (Jesus) as their power source. Greatness is in Him. ***1 John 4:4...***

Flesh vs. Christ

Flesh is a very complicated thing to conquer, especially if you try to conquer it on your own because every time you try to do good things, evil is always present. ***Romans 7:21...*** Humanity is at a constant war. The enemy is very persistent and is always looking for any weaknesses in the defense. The enemy knows exactly what will tempt you the most. ***1 Corinthians 10:13...***

Your flesh will always be in conflict with the Word, and every human will fall short. ***Romans 3:23...*** That is why Jesus died for humanity's sins, so that humanity would not have to live hopeless and defeated in the flesh. He set humanity free from slavery. ***Galatians 5:1... Galatians 5:13-18...*** The flesh loves pleasures. The flesh will fool you into perpetual sin and unhappiness.

Fleshly pleasures are only a mirage. ***Galatians 5:19...*** After the pleasure disintegrates, the person will be left feeling pain in the end. Flesh fools or entices a person into short-lived pleasures. Then, after the pleasure has diminished, the spirit will be left feeling down and dirty. Flesh will leave you disappointed in yourself time after time, even though you know better. Therefore, sin places you back in your worldly mind and out of the Christ mind, further disrupting the meditation and peace for which you have worked hard to acquire. It is a labor to rest in Christ. ***Hebrews 4:11...***

It was by Christ's stripes that you made it through those fleshly sins. Some people have perished from the same sin you survived through. Give thanks and drop sin of iniquity right now, and do not ever turn back because sin leaves you feeling filthy, and your spirit hates it.

Flesh without Christ is doomed, because when Christ died on the cross, humanity's sins died also. **_Romans 7:8..._** The sins of this world inflicted as much excruciating pain on Jesus as the bloody crucifixion because He knew no sin. **_2 Corinthians 5:21..._ _Romans 3:20-22..._** He took on all of the sins of this world and won! **_Romans 7:1-6..._** With Christ in your life, you have been forgiven for your fleshly ways. You are righteous in the sight of God because of the belief in His son, Jesus.

Blessed is the man whose sins the Lord will never count against him. **_Romans 4:8..._** Jesus charged all of humanity's sins to His account. He paid it all! **_Romans 4:6-8..._** Never beat yourself up over things you have done. Just fix it and move on. Repent. **_Romans 8..._ _Romans 7:21-25..._** No one can fulfill the law except for Jesus. Humanity was released from the law by Christ dying on the cross. **_Hebrews 8:6-9..._** You are under the new covenant. Now you are totally under grace. **_Romans 7:4-6..._ _Romans 6:14..._ _John 1:17..._**

The law is like a mirror, showing you everything that is wrong with you. The law is Holy, but it cannot make you Holy. The law is perfect and you are not, but Jesus is. As Jesus is, so is His believers and He is all powerful! Even if you are in jail, you can fix it and be great. Christ makes it available to be great even from behind bars. You just have to believe it. God did it for Joseph. Learn how to let some things go in life and live in the Spirit. You are free from any type of bondage. **_Romans 8:1-4..._**

Nothing in this life is truly yours. You are a steward of everything that you possess. All that you have comes from the Lord. **_James 1:17..._** It is the flesh that holds on to things. The flesh loves confrontations and material things. It feeds on it. If times start to get very rough in your life and it seems like you cannot make it, I urge you to start repeating "Not by might, but by the Spirit of the Lord." **_Zechariah 4:6..._** Keep on repeating that throughout your day.

That is letting your flesh know that you are not depending upon weak, fleshly powers yourself, but you depend upon the Spirit of the Lord instead. Your soul is connected to the Spirit of the Lord. You just have to allow the Spirit to fill you.

Get a special one-on-one relationship with Christ. Train your mouth and mind to be one with Him daily because the enemy is watching you closely. The enemy is watching and anticipating on you to veer off course. Flesh will have you in situations that can set your life back for years. Flesh gets in the way of victory. Keep yourself away from sin by hiding the Word in your heart. You must guard your heart when temptation comes. *__Hebrews 8:10...__*

Many people have let flesh and materials things get in the way to their greatness. Being rich means absolutely nothing without Christ. What is it to gain the whole world, but lose your soul? *__Matthew 16:26...__* Greatness is not about money, sex, or fame. Those are fleshly desires. *__Galatians 5:19-25...__* Greatness is measured upon how many lives you touch and how many people you loved. *__Hebrews 10:24...__*

Greatness is measured whether you trusted in Jesus because if you trust in Him and not the flesh, you are truly great! Choose Christ over flesh and defeat sin where it stands. *__Romans 8:5...__*

Morning by Morning

Every morning you are blessed to wake up. It is a new opportunity to get things right. New life. A rebirth. No matter what had happened yesterday. Let it go. It is behind you. Today is another day to get things turned around in your life. Human life is truly a gift from God. Treat life as the special gift that it is. Some of us are born into poverty and other unfortunate situations. But this is the result of selfish mankind's decisions.

Morning by morning, new mercies I see. **_Lamentations 3:23..._** As soon as you lift up your head off of the pillow, all that you need is already available. You are blessed in any situation with Christ Jesus by your side. Always look to Him to solve your problems. He wants you to depend on Him and His Word. Early in the morning is when the devil likes to strike the most. The devil is stealthy and likes to attack when he feels you are most vulnerable.

Wake up with praise on your heart and in your mouth. Some people believe it is by their own doing they are propelled into success. However, it is truly the Lord working behind the scenes. Just think about it... Nothing could be done without the Savior. **_John 15:5..._** **_Ephesians 1:3..._** If you will just put your trust in Him things will begin to fall in line. **_Jeremiah 39:18..._** You will start to develop a momentum toward success.

Every morning that you wake up, greatness is ahead of you. So do not worry about yesterday's problems or mishaps because morning by morning, you are blessed with a brand-new start.

Persevere

The race is not given to the swift nor to the strong, but to the ones who endure, and endure to the end. _**Ecclesiastes 9:11...**_ It is not about how you start the race. It is all about how you finish the race. Finish the race strong. Every runner in a race will run to win the race. The runners endure strict training and eat the right foods to ensure a healthy body. But they are running for a material crown that will not last. Christians run for a crown that will last forever! _**1 Corinthians 9:24...**_

Do not get weary in doing right. _**Galatians 6:9...**_ Everyone gets tired, but it is the ones who can persevere that will win. Be like running water flowing from a waterfall. Have a never-quit attitude. Never give up when you go through severe times. Keep on pressing toward your goals regardless of what people are thinking or saying about you. _**Philippians 3:13-14...**_ You are on an assignment. You are working on something big.

Your living demonstration of trusting and believing will become inspiration to others. The same people who laughed at your vision will be the same ones who will say they believed in you the entire time. Use your faith like a crafty tool. Use your faith and perseverance to build the life that you want.

Count it all joy when you fall into various trials, knowing that the testing of your faith produces perseverance. _**James 1:2...**_

Trust God

Trust God because Perfect Peace is truly a gift from God. Never fight against peace. Instead, surrender to the Holy Spirit. Rest in it. Your inner spirit must be at peace to bring about peace. Your true strength comes from being peaceful in life. Always seek peace, even when trouble or danger presents itself. ***1 Peter 3:11...*** With God, you already know that your power is unmatched by the enemy. Therefore, you do not have to react in any confrontational manner. You do not have to flex any muscle. You can keep your style and grace. In other words-Keep a calm mind, even though you know that you can cause harm to that person. ***Matthew 5:9...***

"Turn the other cheek," as Jesus says. ***Matthew 5:39...*** The path of the Godly leads to life, so why fear death? ***Proverbs 12:28...*** Your peace and tranquility will strengthen you from within because true power and strength come from within the body, not from reaction. The worldly mind always needs and searches for something to defend. The worldly mind just has to be right in an argument. It just has to have the last word. What are you arguing about or defending? Is it the Word of God? The truth does not have to be debated!

You cannot let the mind and emotions control you. Never let someone else's pain trigger your pain. Remain calm and conscious of every emotion and feeling that you have. This process will allow you to watch your emotions and begin to control them. When you start to feel irritated and angry, do not react to that feeling. Take a few deep breaths and pray. Then, let it go. Put it behind you as quickly as possible. Let it go as if it never happened and trust God. Do not allow your mind to cling to it. Surrender...

Be mindful, instead of mindless. Mindfulness keeps you conscious and in control of the very moment. This process will start to strengthen you from within the mind. This process will also allow you to get to the root of situations. Realize your deficiencies or imperfections and overcome them through the Word. Be mindful of His Word day and night because there are so many forces working against you, those evil forces will try to steal your joy away. **_Joshua 1:8..._ _Ephesians 6:12..._** Trust God and always look at the brighter side of life.

Have a glass-half-full mentality. Letting emotions control decision-making is a bad combination, especially if things do not go as planned or when a disaster strikes. Let the Word of God guide you through. Your steps are ordered by God so trust Him in all of your ways. **_Psalm 37:23..._** Trust God's Word and what He says. Never trust yourself or your own way of thinking. **_Proverbs 3:5..._**

God is all knowing and if an undesirable situation arises, trust Him to work the situation out. Enjoy your Perfect Peace because God is in total control. Trust Him... **_Psalm 33:13-14..._**

Seek ye the Kingdom

"But seek ye first the Kingdom of God, and his righteousness; and all these things shall be added unto you" (**Matthew 6:33**). Seek the kingdom as if you were searching for a lost treasure. **_Proverbs 2:1-6..._** Search and claw for knowledge. God's kingdom has whatever you could want or need in this world.

God said, "He would supply every single need." **_Philippians 4:19..._** He knows how many hairs are on your head. **_Luke 12:7..._** He loves you. He cares about your happiness and feelings. Seek the kingdom for what you want in life and those things will come to pass. Scores of people are looking for marriage and other things that have not come to pass yet. Do not let that disrupt your happiness and peace. Choose to be happy right now no matter what, for He knows what is best for you.

Sometimes He does not come when you want Him to do so, but He will always be there right on time. **_Psalm 27:14..._** Seek the Kingdom of God.

My First Love

Make Jesus your first love. *__Revelation 2:4...__* His love will never fade away from you. *__1 Chronicles 16:34...__* Wait on Him. You will stumble and fall moving on your own. Avoid distractions on your way to the mountaintop. People around you might not quite understand the task that you have at hand, especially in your quest to be great. Not everyone is interested in achieving greatness.

There will be some challenges in front of you that can either make or break you. Do not break! Draw your strength from the Lord your God, your first love. The scriptures says, "That I can do all things through Christ who strengthens me." *__Philippians 4:13...__* He will move the mountain out of the way for you. All you have to do is speak to the mountain. Believe! And it shall be cast into the sea. *__Mark 11:23...__*

Whatever you ask of Him, He will supply. Spend every night with your first love. Never part from Him because He gave His life on the cross for you, then rose on the third day, astonishing everyone that saw Him! *__1 Corinthians 15:4...__* That miraculous event converted Christian killers and despotic rulers to the faith. Constantine is not responsible for Christianity at all. The Roman emperor converted to Christianity in 312 C.E. No one knows but God if Constantine's conversion was sincere or politically motivated. Moreover, the conversion resulted into the end of Christian persecution in his jurisdiction, which set forth a monumental turn in history.

Christ's blood and His love will always make a major change. A difference! Just one touch from the hem of His garment will make you whole. *__Matthew 9:20...__* It was finished with the most graceful display of love in all of Earth's history. ***John 1:14...*** ***Romans 6:23...*** Jesus loved you first.

Situations in life can bring you down, but Jesus will get you back up. Keep on pushing and carry on. It is nothing to a winner like you. Your first love will always triumph on your behalf. Amen...

You Are Not Alone

You may feel like everyone has abandoned you, and you're all alone. But that is not the case at all. You are never alone. *__Hebrews 13:5...__* *__Deuteronomy 31:6...__* God is guiding and watching you the entire way. *__Psalm 32:8...__* God is just clearing a way out for you. He is just removing all of your distractions and obstructions out of your way. So, let things and people go.

Do not hold on to the past or attach yourself to this world. Always continue to move forward. God removes people and things from your life for a reason. Those things are just getting in your way to greatness. Let pain and rejection fuel your greatness because you know that you are not alone. You may be alone physically, but not spiritually.

The spiritual realm is more genuine than the physical realm because the spiritual world birthed the physical world. Get one-on-one with the Spirit. Maybe relationships are not working out the way you want them right now. Just continue to work on yourself through Christ. Learn how to be happy with yourself first. Then you will soon discover that Christ is all that you ever needed in the first place. Jesus will stick closer to you than any brother. *__Proverbs 18:24...__* Everyone else is just icing on the cake, just an extra addition to your already happy and peaceful life.

Learn how to be love because a special someone to make you completely happy is not the answer. That would be putting too much emphasis on the physical. You must first learn how to be happy with just you and God. How can you make someone else happy if you are depressed or confused about your own identity? That is like the blind leading the blind. Learn how to be comfortable in your own skin without anyone else's validation, but God's.

If your mind begin to think hurtful things such as, "He or she does not love me." Or "I am all alone in this world." Take some quiet time and ask yourself a very serious question. Ask yourself, is it really true? Is it really true that no one cares about you? In many cases, the feeling of being alone come from being in someone else's world or business in your mind. The mind can feel lonely when it is focused on someone else's world more than your own.

In all actuality, you are never alone. ***Hebrews 13:5...*** There is more with you than anything! ***2 Kings 6:16...*** God is just clearing out the runway for you, clearing and working things out for you, whom He loves dearly. God is just clearing it out for your good so that you can make a smooth landing on the runway to success and spiritual awakening. The Lord cannot let you land with debris or trash in your way... You are not alone...

Who Are You?

Who are you? The world's model for who you should be is not your true identity. The world is a model of destruction and depression. Let the Word of God shape you into being like clay. Let the Word of God make you into "who you are". When God made us in His image, He was not necessarily talking about the physical stature. God was talking about the Holy Spirit. Your spirit is perfect like His. You are perfect in Christ. ***Colossians 1:28...*** ***Hebrews 12:23...*** When you were born again, born unto Christ, all of your sin died on the cross. ***Romans 6...*** ***Romans 8:1-4...***

Women do not have to act un-Godly to make it rich or to get recognized in life. ***Proverbs 11:22...*** It is vice-versa for the males. It is lifesaving to know who you are, your true identity. It is literally life and death to know who you really came from, because if you do not know yourself or the enemy, you will lose the fight of life every time. You are the seed of God. ***Genesis 1:26-28...*** ***Galatians 3:29...*** Nothing is impossible for you. You are the heir connected to the promise. That is who you are. ***Philippians 4:13...***

Physical appearance and stamina will fade in time. So do not put too much emphasis on that. You cannot make the physical your whole life because it is what's on the inside that really matters. It is what's in the heart that will have any sustainability in this life. The physical body is just a covering for your spirit, like a dress. ***1 Corinthians 15:44-49...*** For example, clothing is a covering for the physical body. But the clothing is not the person. It is just decoration. The physical body is not you as a person, the Spirit is. Focus on the Spirit, which will last forever, and not the physical, which will disintegrate back into the earth. ***Matthew 6:19-22...***

Once upon a time, there was an exponentially gorgeous queen! Queen Marilyn... Everywhere she went, all of the young kings were astonished at the sight of her. Men just worshipped at her feet. A decade later, one day she left the castle to get a quick quenching drink from the stream. As she leaned over to take a sip, she saw her reflection glimmering in the beautiful blue waters. Queen Marilyn started to grow very sad at the sight of her reflection. She had to look twice! The Queen had an epiphany at that very moment, and realized that her looks were fading in time.

The Queen realized at that very moment that she was not going to always be the most beautiful one of them all. All of her happiness and self-esteem had vanished suddenly. Instead of Queen Marilyn just embracing her aging, she fought against it. She never got over that moment at the stream.

The Queen could never be happy with just aging gracefully. Eventually, she died at an early age from a terrible disease. The Queen made the physical her whole life, instead of the Spirit. She made the physical who she was as a person. The moral of this story is to accept what is. Aging gracefully is a blessing. It is a blessing to even get a chance to age.

Queen Marilyn's body shut down on her because she was not happy. She was not trusting and believing in the finished works of Jesus. Your body knows if you love it or not. Love yourself! It does not matter how you look on the outside. That is only the physical. It's the inside that counts. It is the spiritual that makes you who you are. Do not make your body get sick because you don't love it.

Never stand in front of the mirror and belittle yourself. The mirror has no solutions. Let your body know that you love it regardless of how it looks. This process will release the tension that your body has on the inside. Negative thoughts within the brain can actually bring about weight gain and demeaning illusions. Start giving your body positive energy by eating correctly, doing light exercises or stretching. Your positive energy will start to shape your body in the vision that you want. Your body will begin to make a positive shift when you love it.

Show the world who you are from the inside out through Christ. The devil is the enemy and wants you to feel down about yourself. The devil feeds on the lack of confidence, pain, anger, suffering, fear, jealousy, materialism, and the lost identity of humanity. These negative issues are just like steroids to him and his demons.

The devil and his demons literally fly around the earth searching for someone to torment. The devil wants to erase your dreams and identity completely, resulting in erasing your perfect peace; for example, your spirit, mind, physical stature, health, family, business, pet, home, or job. They all can be in "Perfect Peace" if you do it through Christ. *2 Corinthians 5:9-10...*

This world tries to drown out the Lord, especially with all of the added distractions and evil upon the Earth. The Heavens and Earth will fade away, but His Word will stand for eternity. *Matthew 24:35...* That is powerful! The King Creator of the Heavens and the Earth is your Father. Choose to be happy with yourself. Just laugh out of nowhere for no reason at all. You are the child of the Holy King*. Acts 2:36...* That is exactly who you are.

Chapter Two

Perfect Peace

On Your Way to Greatness

We know the End of the Story, Victory is Near

This world can be a peaceful world. In the midst of disaster, you can remain calm. Why? Because you know the end of the story. Victory! Jesus is coming soon. ***Revelation 22:12...*** Would a loving and compassionate father abandon his children? ***John 14:18...*** Jesus is coming back again soon because He said that He was.

We have a very short period of time on Earth. Do not spend your days crying and complaining about situations. Instead, spend your time walking in the Spirit. How can I walk in the Spirit, may you ask? First of all, ask yourself, do my good days outweigh my bad days? Could my situation be worse than what it really is? Nothing is by chance in life.

You have been picked for your situation. Attack problems or life situations like you choose them. God is sovereign and directs the steps of whom delights in Him. ***Psalm 37:23...*** Get it in your mind that greatness is within you. What a man believes in his heart, so is he. ***Proverbs 23:7...*** This means that you must believe in yourself to achieve anything great in life. "I think, therefore I am." Confidence is the key. Hold your head up high because greatness is within you, and victory is near.

Keep your dreams vivid and vibrant. Never let them dwindle away into the sunset. Never lie down when you fall. Always get right back up, dust yourself off and keep on fighting! Keep clawing your way through adversity. Why? Because Jesus is watching you. Do not let Jesus see you with little faith. All you need is the faith of a mustard seed. A mustard seed is a very tiny seed. ***Matthew 17:20...*** Always remember, you move trees and mountains around here! ***Mark 11:23...*** You know the end of the story. Victory is near...

Faith

"So then faith cometh by hearing, and hearing by the word of God" (*Romans 10:17 KJV*). Faith: Complete trust in God and His Word. Faith makes you righteous in the sight of God. *Romans 4:7-25...* "Now Faith is the substance of things hoped for and the evidence of things not seen" (*Hebrews 11:1 KJV*). Hallelujah!

"For by grace are we saved through faith; and not that of yourselves. It is the gift of God. Not of works, lest any man should boast" (*Ephesians 2:8-9).* Grace is inexplicably amazing! Grace is the unmerited/undeserved favor of God. It removes burdens and obliterates yokes. *Isaiah 10:27... Galatians 4:6-7... Galatians 5:1-6...* Faith takes hold of the blessings of God. By grace the blessings of God were made available. *Romans 5:1-2...*

There is one thing that Jesus cannot do and that is to lie. Jesus won't lie to humanity. If faith is put in Him, lives can and will be transformed. You experience God through your faith. Walking in the Spirit feels great. *Galatians 3:14...* Some people may feel that you have to be perfect to walk in the Spirit, to do everything right. But if that were the case, no one would be able to walk in the Spirit. It's by "Grace".

"For all have sinned and fall short of the glory of God" (*Romans 3:23 KJV).* But He still feeds, and takes very good care of us. Jesus will take care of His own. *Matthew 6:26...* Have faith that can move the unmovable, and faith that can see the invisible. *Romans 4:17...* Faith can conquer anything!

To The Ends of the Earth

To the ends of the Earth-God will find you and will supply your every need. *__Philippians 4:19...__* The Lord will deliver you no matter where you are. *__Psalm 97:3-10...__* "The Heavens declare the glory of the Lord, and the firmament shows His handiwork" (*Psalm 19:1 KJV).*

There are more stars in the sky than the grains of sand on every beach on Earth. According to Wikipedia, the Milky Way galaxy contains approximately four hundred billion stars and at least a hundred billion planets. Wow! What a mighty God we serve! God's handiwork will always leave you in awe.

Watching nature always displays God's loving affection to all walks of life. *__Job 35:11...__* Everything on Earth has a cycle, a season. Humanity has a season also in life, but our season may not last just for a few months. Seasons last as long as God wants them to last. Animals and humans depend on the different seasons to survive. Animals store up food and even hibernate. It is amazing how God orchestrated these marvelous cycles.

God created an inestimable amount of life. New creatures and wonders are being discovered every day. Every animal or insect has their needs met with a special intricate design. *__Job 12:7...__* The animals do not plant, harvest, or store food in barns, but the heavenly Father still feeds them. So you can rest for sure that God will supply your every need. Because if He will take care of the wildlife, He will surely take care of you. *__Matthew 6:25-34...__* The Lord will make manna rain from the heavens for you. All the way to the ends of the Earth... *__Psalm 78:23-25...__*

Always look to God in every situation. God will direct your path. Even when you are in a dark season. Be patient. Let God be your truth and the light. **_John 14:6..._** To everything there is a season. Wait ye on the Lord. **_Ecclesiastes 3:1... Zephaniah 3:8..._** He already knows what you need, before you even need it. All the way to the ends of the Earth, your needs will be met. So do not worry at all.

Search for Him

Search for God in every situation. One morning I woke up feeling hopeless and wanted to complain, frustrated at all of my failures in life. But then I caught myself and started to focus on the almighty God, the God who has sent the Son of Man to save us from the enemy. ***John 3:16...***

The enemy is coming relentlessly every day to eat and devour the flesh. ***1 Peter 5:8...*** But the devil and his demons have already been defeated! The enemy has stumbled and fallen, 2,000 years ago at the cross. ***Jeremiah 20:11...*** The battle is not yours, it is the Lord's. ***2 Chronicles 20:15...***

Furthermore, when the feeling of frustration, complaining, or hopelessness come about, look for God's power to deliver you. He will give you the hope that you need. Hopeless means faithless. Believe in God's ability, and not the physical. Believe in things not seen yet, and call them out as if though they were. ***Romans 4:17...*** It is not your ability that will get you to the Promised Land or your destination in life, so do not get frustrated. ***Hebrews 12:22-24...*** It is the strength and direction that the Lord gives you. Search for Him.

He is Coming Soon

No man knows the day or hour that the Lord is coming back to the Earth. But it is always very refreshing to know that "The Son of Man" is coming back soon. *__Hebrews 9:28...__ __1 Thessalonians 4:14...__ __Matthew 24:30-36...__* Riding through the clouds He will come. *__Revelation 1:7...__* There will be many signs before His return. Society will be in terrible times, and people will be lovers of themselves. *__2 Timothy 3:1-5...__* Does that sound familiar? Also knowledge will be increased. *__Daniel 12:4...__*

With today's technology and negligence, it will only be a very short period of time before humanity would destroy God's beautiful creation. Earth's history is in its very last days as we know it. The "Messianic Age" is coming very soon. Jesus promised that He will save all of His followers from evil and disaster. All of the dead will rise in Christ. *__1 Thessalonians 4:16-17...__ __John 5:28-29...__*

Jesus will ransom His believers from the grave. *__Hosea 13:14...__* All of your atoms will be put back together again. There will be a major transformation to the DNA of Christ's followers. The believers' bodies will be transformed to be just like Christ's glorious body. (The Light Body) *__Philippians 3:20-21...__* The meek will inherit the Earth. (The Golden Race) *__Matthew 5:5-10...__*

Death and sin came through one man, Adam. Eternal life came through the blood of the Lamb, Jesus Christ. *__1 Corinthians 15:21-22...__* Earth is not our home. It is just a passing place. *__1 Peter 2:11...__ __Hebrews 13:14...__* Jesus's disciples asked, "What will be the signs of the end of the age?" (The Golden Age) The age when the "Golden One" shall rise again. *__Matthew 24:3-44...__ __Revelation 20:1-6...__*

The signs Jesus spoke about are transpiring at this very moment. The end times will be like the days of Noah, Jonah, or Lot. ***Luke 17:26-30...*** ***Matthew 12:38-45...*** He is coming soon. These are just the labor pains of the Earth. Listen to her moan and scream for mercy. The negligent humans on this Earth have inflicted a tremendous amount of pain on her. Mother Earth screams with her fierce hurricanes, earthquakes, tsunamis, raging wildfires, and floods. But there is much more to come.

Stay aware of what is going on in the world. Be conscious. The devil wants you to be totally distracted, partying, and indulging in entertainment when the Savior comes. ***Genesis 19:5-12...*** ***Romans 1:18-32...*** The devil knows that his time of evil reign is almost over. ***Luke 8:28...*** Looking for Jesus is the last thing that the devil wants humanity to do. That's why there is so much entertainment and distractions now. The time is near. Today's cell phones have more technology than the space shuttle Apollo that traveled to the moon in the year 1969.

There are systems in place that record or manipulate all of the information in the world. This system is a setup for the anti-Christ to control everyone's information. It is here now. There will be signs in the stars that have never taken place on the Earth coming very soon. ***Luke 21:25-36...*** Jesus said, "So when all these things begin to happen, stand and look up, for your salvation is near" (***Luke 21:28 NLT***).

NASA has confirmed that the solar system has begun a major transformation. Every planet in our solar system is experiencing a major change in their atmospheres. It is not just Earth experiencing extreme climate changes. There is an interplanetary climate change permeating throughout the whole solar system. A very special event is coming soon. Pay attention! The devil wants your attention to be on social media, reality shows, and etc.... He wants you to tarry on and concentrate on meaningless things. Anything that does not add to the Kingdom of God is meaningless and time wasted. When Jesus returns, it will be the most impactful event that ever took place upon the Earth. ***Acts 1:11...*** ***Matthew 24:29-35...***

The devil wants you to be totally oblivious towards his evil plan for you. Remember, his job is to distract and devour. This world is dark for the ones who do not know the "Prince of Peace". Without Christ's protection, this world is filled with misery and relentless, hideous demons. Christians are to be the radiant light for the darkness of this world. *__Matthew 5:14...__* *__Matthew 6:22...__* *__John 8:12...__* *__Luke: 11:33...__* If Jesus is not your Savior, you will be consumed by the enemy.

Wait on Jesus because He is coming soon. Jesus has gone and prepared a place where there are many mansions. *__John 14:2...__* So be ready. Make sure your heart is right. He is coming soon, like a thief in the night. *__1 Thessalonians 5:2...__*

The Devil Is a Liar

The devil is a liar. You are forgiven! The blood of Christ cleanses you from all sin. *1 John 1:7...* *1 John 3:9...* The devil has no control over you with the mind of Christ. Your sin is dead when you are in Jesus. *Romans 6:1-7...* When God looks at you, all He see is His son Jesus on the inside of you. The devil and his demons are in collusion to devour you.

Take the narrow path through the gates, for the wide gate and broad road leads to destruction. *Matthew 7:13...* This means it is very necessary not to do what everyone else is doing. They are being deceived. You may wonder sometimes, why do things keep happening to you? Or why do bad things happen to good people? You may say, "I love Jesus." Or you may say, "I love the Lord." Or "Jesus has forgotten all about me." In this world, we are all feeling the consequences of Adam and Eve's sin in the Garden of Eden. *Romans 5:15-19...* *Genesis 3:1-24...*

Just remember that trouble does not last always. *James 1:2-4...* Your best days are right in front of you. Your vision determines your future. Adversity can serve as the Lord's way to get you in line with Him, to wake you up, to get you conscious. The only way to obtain consciousness is to know you have been unconscious. So do not let the devil lie to you, and get in your mind. Stay alert and on fire in your heart for Christ. *Luke 24:32...*

Humans were placed upon the Earth to serve God and enjoy His peace. Humans were placed upon the Earth to join the Angels in defeating the devil and his grotesque demons. *Revelation 12:7-9...* Do not be a bystander in Christ. Hold up the bloodstained banner! Let your light shine and join the fight! *__2 Corinthians 10:3-5...__* *__Luke 11:33...__* Spread the gospel of Jesus's love and supernatural power throughout the planet. Find a way to pass your light on to future generations. Let's expose the enemy for the liar that he is. "Submit yourselves, then, to God. Resist the devil, and he will flee from you" (*James 4:7 NIV*). You have been forgiven 2,000 years ago. *__1 John 2:2...__* Don't fall from grace believing what the devil says. The devil is a liar! *__Galatians 5:4-6...__*

Chapter Three

Perfect Peace

On Your Way to Greatness

Chip Away to Greatness

Chip away to greatness. Greatness does not come about overnight. Rest in the finished works of Christ. ***Proverbs 14:23...*** This means it is okay to work hard on your vision, but just do not worry about the outcome. You cannot be afraid to have a vision. A vision is a portrait of possibility sent by God. Even if your vision is abnormal, do not be afraid to utilize it because God does not do anything ordinary. Get intimate with Him. Make Him exclusive in your life. God knew you before you were in your mother's womb. He knew you before the world was even formed. ***Ephesians 1:4...***

God has given you an assignment to perform. Never sleep away your hour of opportunity. ***Proverbs 10:5...*** He loves you more than human comprehension. You are not a normal person. You were known billions, perhaps trillions, of years ago! So won't He know your direction and what's best for you? Stay strong, do not get weary in chipping away at greatness. Jesus will armor you with everything you need on the way. ***Philippians 4:19...***

It is not you making things happen. It is not you making the wind blow. It is the power of the Lord that works through you that makes things happen. It is the unseen that is most essential in life. God would even send a raven to feed you to fulfill your greatness. Wow! A raven? All the way to the ends of the Earth, He will find you! Out of the ordinary is how God works. Ravens are scavenger birds. Carrion is its primary food source. The raven would normally devour the bread quickly before it would get to you. ***1 Kings 17:6...*** Now, that is love for God to assist you all the way to greatness.

Suppress all worrying. God will equip you on your journey. Keep on chipping away, all the way to the top for greatness.

We Are at War

Put on the whole armor of God so that you will be able to stand against the wiles of the devil. Our struggle, your fight, is not against flesh and blood. _**Ephesians 6:11-18...**_ That means your enemy is not the person that offends you or makes you angry. The true fight is against demons and evil forces in high places, seeking whom they may devour. _**1 Peter 5:8... 2 Corinthians 10:4-5...**_

Separate your emotions from all decision-making. The enemy wages war with the mind. Use your Christ mind when making decisions. As soon as you start making decisions with the mind of Christ, the enemy will send out a missile of attack to distract you, trying to fill your mind with egotistical thoughts. The devil's job is to knock you off course, to make you revert back into the old you, your old mind. The sinful, egotistical mind is at war with the mind of Christ. Put on the whole armor of God because no weapon formed against you can prosper. No weapon. None at all. _**Isaiah 54:17...**_

Never let the old mind sneak back into your life after you have renewed your mind for Christ. The key word here is to "Renew". To renew your mind means to restore your mind to its original condition because you cannot renew anything that you've never had in the first place. For example, you cannot renew a subscription to a magazine or newspaper you've never had. This means you've had the mind of Christ before the fall of Adam.

How do I renew my mind, you may ask? _**Romans 12:2...**_ First, you have to be immersed in Christ. Immersed in Christ means the belief in Him and God's Word because if any man be in Christ, he is a new creature.

The old ways are passed away and the new is here. (The old way of thinking patterns, strongholds, or excessive thinking.) *2 Corinthians 5:17...*

"The mind makes a good servant, but it makes a terrible master." When you are immersed in Christ, the way you picture the world will change drastically. The war of life will begin to turn in your favor. This world will not be so bad or hurtful anymore. The hostility of the world and its actions will cease to have an effect on you.

And lastly, you have to keep your mind on Jesus without ceasing to be renewed. *1 Thessalonians 5:17...* That is how you keep your Perfect Peace in the time of warfare. That is how you become spiritually and strategically war-ready for anything! *Isaiah 26:3...* You will be ready for whatever comes your way. Not by might but by the Spirit of the Lord will make you become war-ready.

Eat

Then Jesus said unto them, "Verily, verily, I say unto you, Except ye eat the flesh of the Son of Man, and drink of His blood, ye have no life in you" (**John 6:53 KJV**). Jesus answered, "It is written: 'Man shall not live on bread alone, but on every word that comes out of the mouth of God'" (**Matthew 4:4 NIV**).

This means you do not just need edible food, but what is most essential to eat is the Word of God, your Spiritual food. You do this by meditating and digesting God's Word. Meditating and digesting God's Word gives you peace and rest for your soul. **_Joshua 1:8..._** The Word is food for your soul, which cures all kinds of sicknesses and diseases within the body. Peace and hope within the mind changes the body's whole molecular structure. Your emotions directly affect every cell in the body.

The more you eat the Word, the more peaceful and comfortable you will become. The Holy Word is full of His promises. The Word is God, so why would anyone ever be down in the dumps? **_John 1:1..._** Take Jesus with you every day, all day. Speak only of positive things because after all, it is what comes out of the mouth that defiles a man. Things that come from the mouth come from the heart. **_Matthew 15:11..._** **_Matthew 12:34..._** Physical food will go through the stomach and through the body. Spiritual food will enter the body to reside.

Eat the Word because you are what you eat. The Word is your power pellet! Let the Word of God work in your life. Then, get out of the way and enjoy the ride. Rest. Jeremiah said in the Bible that the Word is like fire burning, deep down in his bones. **_Jeremiah 20:9..._** The Word of the

Lord was scintillating and overwhelming to Jeremiah. Jeremiah could not hold the Word in; he had to spew it out! Speak and eat the Word constantly because, ultimately, what you say is what you will receive in life.

You would not eat anything every day that you knew resulted in food poisoning. That is insane! Eating the world's food will definitely lead to sickness and pain every day. You must eat your super-substantial bread. Super-substantial bread is the Word of God. (Bread from the Highest) The daily bread of God nourishes the physical and the spiritual simultaneously.

It is not wise to speak upon things which you do not truly believe or know. Just don't do it. Even if you are joking. ***James 1:26...*** Saying things like, "You are killing me." Or things like "If I do not get this or that item, I will just die." Your words literally mean everything. ***Matthew 12:36...*** Always speak and think positive through any circumstance. Your words represent your thoughts. "If you change your words, you can change your life."

Let your words be the pen of a masterful writer for your life. ***Psalm 45:1...*** Choose your words very wisely because they release spiritual forces. Eating the Word puts joy on your heart. Eating the Word of God brings prosperity and peace to your life. Eat it!

Hold On

Hold on to your faith, my sisters and brothers. God is with you. _**Isaiah 41:10...**_ Never get weary in doing right and working hard. _**Galatians 6:9...**_ The Lord has already prepared a place for you. _**Deuteronomy 31:8...**_ Your faith strengthens from hearing the Word every day. _**Romans 10:17...**_ "So do not throw away your confidence; it will be richly rewarded" (**Hebrews 10:35**). Hold on and never give up.

Keep your faith working out in the field until what you request from the Lord manifests itself in your life. Things may be rough right now, but hold on. Relief is coming soon. Never listen to the devil because he is a perpetual liar. He may be telling you things that are hurtful to your spirit.

Things like... "Hold on for what?" "No one loves you." "You will never be anything in life." "You are a failure." "You are all alone." "Your situation will never get better." "Jesus does not love you." "There is no God, because if there were, your life would be better or perfect." Those are only some of the vicious lies of the enemy. Those lies are humorous to the believer in Christ because Christians know if God is for them, nothing can stand in their way. _**Romans 8:31...**_

Many people commit suicide because they feel hopeless and cornered with no escape. Many of them may feel like no one understands what they are going through. _**1 Peter 5:9...**_ Depression is a very serious sickness in the mind. Depression can feel like a 1,000-pound weight on your shoulders. Depression and compulsive thinking is a sickness that creates fear and doubt. Depression and compulsive thinking torments the mind over and over again. Depression can be a very dark place without the Truth and the Light. But Jesus will shine His light on the darkest horizon. So hold on!

Pills will not necessarily be the answer to a mind problem. Because they may only temporarily suppress the depression or deepen it, the pills never get to the root of the problem. A problem of feeling hopeless is completely in the mind. There is always a solution. There is always hope. Hold on!

Never put your emphasis or trust in a worldly mind. A worldly mind creates strongholds in your psyche. Strongholds are contrary to God. *Philippians 4:8...* Step out of the mind to defeat it. This process of stepping out of the mind will allow the mind to have no power against you. The personification of the worldly mind is a hindrance because a worldly mind thinks of worldly ways and strategies, worldly ways and strategies that only result in more pain and stress. *1 John 2:15...*

Use your imagination to step out of your mind and right into peace. Imagine yourself stepping out of the body and observing your emotions. Get to where the situations and so-called problems of this world do not bind you anymore. It is the attachment of this world that brings about suffering. Let the world go and "hold on" to Jesus. Attach yourself to the Holy Spirit, where liberty is everlasting. This will allow you to become strong in the Spirit. *Ephesians 6:10...* Subsequently, depression and compulsive thinking will be obsolete.

Get your mind in sync with Christ. He conquered the whole world. Salvation, peace, purity, patience, righteousness, and compassion, is in Him. *2 Corinthians 3:17...* The Holy Lamb lives within you, so you have more than enough strength to hold on. *Galatians 2:20...* The devil wins if he can shatter your steadfastness and kill your confidence in God. The devil wants you to over-think everything instead of holding on and resting so the Lord can work. Count it a victory for the devil if you ever capitulate or give up on your dreams.

When it is time to go to heaven and the devil is revealed, how small and insignificant he was will be made evident. You will think, "Is this the little devil that I let torment me in the mind all of my life?" Never let any situation going on in the world kill your confidence in Christ. *Colossians 2:16-19...* Hold on, my sisters and brothers.

He Is Going to Wipe Away Your Tears

He will wipe all of your tears away. All of your tears right now are just temporary. ***Revelation 21:4...*** You will not have to cry anymore because He is coming back again. Do not get it confused, though. I am not talking about your mate or spouse wiping your tears away. I am talking about the greatest gift of all Jesus Christ, of course! ***Corinthians 9:15 KJV... Romans 6:23...*** He is a constant friend. A journey with Jesus is a life worth living. What a marvelous Savior we have in Jesus.

As humans/flesh, we are going to make mistakes in life. Learn how to forgive yourself for falters. God has already forgiven you for them. ***Hebrews 8:12...*** Situations and conditions in life can change in a heartbeat. Life is but a vapor. You do not even know what will happen tomorrow. ***James 4:14...*** So, be happy today. Your whole life can be changed and transformed overnight. Therefore, do not place your center of attention on the problem. Placing attention on problems will only slow you down.

If life is but a vapor? It is time to move in the right direction now, yesterday, not tomorrow. You cannot let your dirty past cripple your great future. Your center of attention should be on greatness, love, and peace. ***2 John 1:3...*** Focus on the right now. The right now takes control of your past immediately.

Let your mistakes and doubters ignite your future. Let adversity enflame your ambition. Show everyone who you really are. You are an image of Christ. Call on Him, and He will be there right away. Belief and trust is the currency of the Kingdom. Without trust, no transaction can be made. Disasters may come, but no situation will ever be more than you can bear. Everything is going to be all right. Jesus promised that He will wipe every tear away from your eyes...

Chapter Four

Perfect Peace

On Your Way to Greatness

Real Love

Oftentimes, people may feel like they know what real love is. My Spiritual leader always says, "Love is, what love does." And that is true. Love is an action word. You show love, not talk it. There is one thing in life that every living thing needs, and that is the undeniable power of love. ***Psalm 145:9...***

Love is the highest vibrational energy in the universe. Love transcends space and time. A newborn baby would die without the loving touch of a human. Humanity would not even exist without love. God's love for us is the reason why we even breathe. ***Colossians 1:16...*** The Almighty God orchestrates the rhythmic waves of the oceans that keep us alive.

If the sun deviated a little bit forward, it would destroy everything on Earth. If the sun deviated a little bit backwards, it would freeze everything on Earth. Now, that is real love to place us in the perfect area for the emergence of life. These perfect conditions for life cannot be by chance. Science dubbed these perfect conditions as the "Goldilocks zone". He loves us. Each one of us.

Jesus's love will cover you for eternity. ***Romans 6:1-23...*** The blood of Jesus makes the Angel of Death pass right over you. Death occurs when the body is no longer useful, or when the individual's assignment is over. It is His "Real Love" keeping you alive every day. God's inhale and exhale is the reason why all living things breathe. The fractal vibration energy that the Lord generates holds all things in place. If the Lord were to cease the fractal vibration, everything ever made would collapse back into a single mass, smaller than the ballpoint of a pen.

You are completely covered by love. So if you are feeling all alone and not loved, that couldn't be further from the truth. Jesus, the compassionate said, "That He will never leave you, or forsake you." **_Hebrews 13:5... Deuteronomy 31:6... John 14:18..._** Real love is never mean or disrespectful. Love is patient and kind. **_1 Corinthians 13:4-8..._** Negative energy or animosity is like a deadly contagious disease. It spreads around very rapidly and affects everyone.

"Ubuntu" is real. Ubuntu has been proven scientifically through quantum physics. "Ubuntu" is a word from the Nguni language, and it has several meanings. The root meaning of Ubuntu is the connectedness that exists or should exist between humanity. We are all interconnected. Humanity is even connected to the stars in the sky. The whole universe is a gargantuan cosmic web. So spread real love throughout the universe. God's command is to walk in love. **_1 John 4:7... 2 John 1:6..._**

Only people that carry pain on the inside create pain for others and themselves. Real love arises from within the heart and beyond the worldly mind. So-called love with a person can bring just as much sadness as joy, especially after the excitement is gone. Some people get into relationships for their own selfish reasons. For example, some people get into relationships for control, companionship from loneliness, manipulation, sexual desires, physical appearance, or revenge from past relationships. Their motives are only in their favor. Only their best interests are in mind. With those types of motives, love can turn into hate very quickly.

No one is everything to you, except for Christ Jesus. It is very dangerous to put so much emphasis in someone. Putting too much emphasis on a person will lead to total disaster. Never secure your happiness on people or material things. If you do, down you will go! **_Proverbs 11:28..._** Jesus replied, "Love the Lord your God with all of your heart and with all of your soul and with all your mind" (**_Matthew 22:37 NIV_**). Also, "Love your neighbor as yourself." "Everyone should hold on to these two commandments," Jesus said. **_Matthew 22:39..._** Your father in heaven loves you. He loved you first. Now, that is the example of real love. **_1 John 4:16... John 3:16..._**

In This Life

In this life, we will endure pain and sorrow. In this life, we experience pestilence, wars, and murders. Loved ones may die and leave us all alone. Disappointments and troubles are sure to come. In this life, things go wrong very often. We live in a world full of evil ideals. But even through all of that, Jesus brings good news. Trouble does not last always, and pain is only temporary. ***Psalm 9:9-10...*** It may seem like the turmoil that you are going through will never end. Weeping only endures for the night, but joy comes in the morning light. ***Psalm 30:5...***

When all hell breaks loose, you have to be able to stand on the promises of Jesus and believe that He will do just what He said. Jesus said, "If you love me, keep my commandments." Then, He will ask the Father in Heaven to give you another advocate. The Spirit of Truth will be your advocate to help you and will be with you forever in this life. ***John 14:15-21...***

Do not let your hearts be troubled about the things of this world. Leave this world and its problems behind. ***John 14:1-4...*** There is a whole other world prepared for you. Jesus has already prepared it. What must be understood is that Christians work at a supernatural advantage in this life.

Christians have a nice, safe place to reside when disaster strikes. ***Isaiah 4:6...*** For example, there is a baby that is crying immensely, and no one can pacify the infant until the mother comes in, and the baby lays its head on the mother's breast. The baby is immediately content because the infant knows it's safe and sound. The infant's instinct knows that the mother is the biological parent. It is the same way with Jesus.

Let Jesus be your shelter. Lay your head on Him when times get rough. In this life, let Jesus be your storm/strong tower. ***Proverbs 18:10...***

Hold your head up high and put that smile back on your face. In this life, do not let anybody or anything steal your joy. As I said before, life is but a vapor. Why spend it all sad and defeated? Let us live to win in this life. Very soon there will be a new Heaven and Earth where we will not even need the sun to shine its beautiful rays. ***Revelation 21:1...***The Lord Jesus's power will illuminate the whole Earth. ***Revelation 22:5...*** So in this life, focus on the Savior. In this life, be great!

Food

Taste and see that the Lord is good. ***Psalm 34:8...*** Food and water are not the only sources that are keeping the body alive. It is actually the Word of God that we digest keeping us alive. Furthermore, without the Word of God, there would not be any light source to even support life or food. ***Genesis 1:3...*** It is literally the Word keeping us alive every day. Not bread alone. It would be better to die without food than to die without the Word of God. ***John 1:1-5...***

The Word of God is what makes life worth living. It is the Word of the Lord that places you in His Perfect Peace. The Word is essential and is needed daily. This world tries to drown out the Word with carnal thinking and commentary. Ninety-nine percent of television is nonreligious. That is why the world is hurting so much as a society. Every day there are murders, rapes, and suicides. ***Romans 1:28-32...*** No one even trusts each other anymore. Everyone is on guard and defensive because so many people are not eating their spiritual food. ***Psalm 119:103...*** They are not eating the Word of God.

Bad things may happen to good people, but the Word of God will give them the strength to stand through any storm or situation. Eat your spiritual food every day. ***Matthew 15:11...*** Let us change the world with one Christ-like being at a time. ***Philippians 2:1-4...***

Find the Real You

Take an intricate look at-and within-yourself, a self-inventory. _**2 Corinthians 13:5-10...**_ Observe all of your tendencies very closely. What are your constant unconscious, habitual acts? Condemning them or getting agitated is not the way to correct them. Just observe them, write them down, and change whatever it is. Never live your life on autopilot. Stay aware at all times.

Oftentimes, people try to emulate others to feel relevant. _**1 Corinthians 11:1...**_ People also imitate others to feel validated in a hostile and confusing world. The way a person walks or talks all comes from whom they desire themselves to be. With all of the added social media and entertainment, true self-identity can be lost. Many people are dependent on getting likes on social media and other avenues to validate them, resulting in their doing wild and crazy things to get recognized or seen.

Television is a very powerful force. Television is a very unscrupulous, controlled perception to the world. However the world wants society to behave, television or videos displays it. The deception is real. Television and all types of media play endless tricks on societies' consciousness. This is another avenue where evil or the cabal is greatly glorified. The enemy wants you to be thoroughly entertained and distracted.

Satan uses entertainment to distract humanity from the real issues in society. The devil does not like people who think deeply from within because deep thinkers challenge the status quo and the evil of this world. Television has been used to perpetuate hate all over the world. It makes enemies of people who have never met and continues to spread viscous lies.

True self-identity can be completely lost when other people are imitated, especially other people with giant egos that are lost themselves. The egotistical, worldly mind judges everything and always has an argument. The egotistical, worldly mind only takes away from true happiness and searches for conflicts. The egotistical, worldly mind is the enemy. In fact the egotistical, worldly mind is not even the real you. It is not your true identity. The egotistical, worldly mind is just trying to fit in with the rest of the unconscious world.

Too much bad entertainment can train your mind to work against you because your thoughts would be of other peoples' and not of Christ. Humanity's ideals are flawed. Follow and imitate the "Flawless One". (Jesus Christ) Today could be your last day upon the Earth. Would you want to spend it being you, or someone else?

You are a spirit being made by God. What spirit are you following? Is it a spirit of selfishness and mammon? This is a disastrous combination to live within. Your spirit will never be satisfied with that combination inside of you. Mammon and selfishness will always crave more and more. They will never be satisfied with how you already are.

Mammon will always tell you that you do not have enough in life, and selfishness will never allow you to spread love and give to humanity generously. Mammon and selfishness can only survive in a worldly-minded individual. The worldly mind will never allow you to live in the moment and enjoy who you are through Christ today. _**1 John 2:15-16...**_ Enjoy your life whether you have a little or an abundance. When you imitate Christ, worldly desires does not mean anything and serving humanity will mean everything. Imitate Him to find the real you.

Make sure you are very careful who you emulate through music or any other avenues. Lucifer was the Archangel of music and entertainment before his fall from heaven. He was a walking, talking, musical instrument. He had music pipes built right within his body. God created him that way for His glory. _**Ezekiel 28:13-15...**_ _**Revelation 12:9...**_ Not all entertainment or music is bad, of course. If the song makes you feel good, positive, and inspired, then it is a good song. There are more songs written about Jesus today than any other figure in the history of mankind. God is still in total control, He never lost it. Humans just lost their real true identity by imitating other people.

Humanity is mimicking the false reality the world portrays. There is an enemy trying to sneak his way into humanity's cars and homes unnoticed, then eventually sneaking his way into the minds of people. Through music and trillions of other ways, the devil is at work. The devil promotes hatred and violence through song. He wants to make it look very compelling to be those individuals. It's his specialty. This is where he is greatly glorified.

Some famous musical artists have even admitted that they take on different spirits when they perform. The question is, what kind of spirit? *1 John 4:1...* You should be able to tell by the lyrics and dance routine. Luciferianism and other satanic practices are being used throughout entertainment worldwide. *2 John 1:7...* Take some time and do some research on your own. Then you may soon realize that Satan is very much alive and still up to his old tricks. *1 John 3:8...*

Do not be misled to hate and to do other corruptive things; for example, trying to be like someone who sounds or looks "cool" through entertainment, flashing a bunch of money with girls or men all over them. *Matthew 6:24...* Sounds good? Those things do not matter to someone that is desiring to be more like Jesus. That is not what greatness is about in the Kingdom. Actually, it is mirroring the same symbol of the gruesome demon mammon. The demon of mammon is depicted sitting on a throne with gold and riches all around him. *Ecclesiastes 2:2-11...* Mammon is only one of the many demons or evil spirits in high places. *Ephesians 6:12...*

Jesus protects His people every day from getting devoured by those evil spiritual forces. *Psalm 68:19...* The spiritual realm is more authentic than the physical realm. The spiritual world has an extensive amount of entities that have never been created on Earth. There is a major battle going on in the spiritual world. There are demons after your soul to annihilate your identity. Those demons want your Christ mind to be obsolete and to divert your focus of attention towards glitz and glamour.

People must watch very closely who they emulate in music videos, and other forms of entertainment. As I have said before, mammon is extensively glorified in them. As a matter of fact, those people are only trying to obtain the happiness and joy that Jesus has already supplied inside. You can have a party everyday with Jesus. He is the most compelling or "coolest" one of them all, after a little time is spent with Him. He supplies elaborate knowledge and insight that is far more valuable than riches. ***Proverbs 8:10-11...***

Jesus from Nazareth shapes and conforms you into a "first class" human being. He supplies you first-class knowledge and intelligence that no school can teach. In Christ, you will be able to control your mind and senses. You will also be purpose-driven, clean, truthful, tolerant of others, uncomplicated, and very intuitive. Be whom God created you to be. God gave all of humanity an individuality. Never compare yourself with others and the possessions they have. Every blessing has someone's name on it. God will not help you be someone else. We are all unique to God, and He loves us. He made you to be you, not someone else.

You are great in your own right. Everyone has special gifts that come from God. ***James 1:17...*** Therefore, that means we all have favor. ***1 Peter 4:10-11...*** Never forget who you are and why you were placed upon the Earth. Not knowing who you are is a never-winning way to live. Your spirit will suffer as a result of lost identity. Find the real you. The only way to truly be yourself is through Jesus Christ. ***2 Corinthians 3:3-11...*** Never fool yourself. You are not strong or wise enough to achieve greatness or peace without Him.

Take life one day at a time. With Christ you will find your "real true identity". Walking with Christ is the only way to find your true self. The real you, not someone else. ***Colossians 2:9-10... 1 John 3:1-2...***

Life Goes On

Pick up the pieces. Lift up your majestic head. Have supreme confidence and know that you are the child of the Holy King. Nothing can stop you. Nothing can ever defeat you. Life goes on. Loved ones may pass away, but you will see them again. The dream world is your link to the loved ones that have passed away. Just ask the Lord for dreams of them. After that, just relax your mind and heart. Then before you know it, your prayers will be answered. But still, life goes on.

People may turn their backs on you. But that is okay because you have Jesus, the comforter, and you can talk with Him all night. He won't ever get tired of you. Friends may desert you, but Jesus will be there late in the midnight hour. _**Deuteronomy 31:8...**_ Learn how to turn pain and disappointments into total blessings. Learn how to thrive in the face of disappointments. You just cannot lose with Jesus by your side. He is the perfect teammate. It is impossible to lose. _**Psalm 37:28...**_

Those with a troubled heart, I have great news. _**John 14:27...**_ Jesus conquered it all on the cross for you, so that you may rise up to greatness today. _**Revelation 1:18... John 20:1-19...**_ Never let roadblocks discourage you at all. Trials may come, but keep on moving. Life goes on.

Get all that you can out of your life today. Only the dead remain in the same place. The dead know nothing. Furthermore, while you are alive, always move forward. Move forward for your loved ones. There is no time to remain idle or move backwards. _**Ecclesiastes 9:1-7...**_ Life is too precious and short for that. Looking backwards only makes you veer off course. It is senseless to try to walk straight looking backwards. Eventually, you will crash into something. The only time it is okay to look backwards is when you look back to see how far God has brought you. Life goes on... **_Luke 9:62..._**

Once upon a time there was a bird named Clarence. Clarence lived in a pond with a flock of ducks. All of the ducks were always laughing and ridiculing him until one day, the pond suddenly dried up. Clarence had to make a decision. He had to decide if he should leave with the flock, or find another domain. Clarence decided to go off on his own because he was tired of trying to fit in and of being mocked all the time.

So Clarence opened up his silky feathers and soared with the wind beneath his wings. But while he was in flight, he saw his reflection in the water below. Clarence thought he was seeing things. He could not believe his eyes. Clarence was actually a beautiful trumpeter swan. Clarence realized right then that he was not a duck at all!

With the wind beneath his wings, he soared to another nearby pond with emerald waters. The luminous emerald pond was filled with other beautiful swans. Soon after Clarence landed in the new pond, the swans in the emerald pond declared Clarence as the most beautiful and graceful one of them all. The moral of the story is that you will have to move on from people that are contrary to your greatness. Life must go on.

Some of the people that you want to be a part of your journey may desert or laugh at you. Do not be distracted by that. Move on from people who distract you from your greatness. Some people will never perceive your greatness and will always point out your faults. A good friend should only add to your successes and confidence. That is what friends are for. They should not ever disparage your greatness. Constructive criticism is great from someone with good intentions. You just cannot let people that are not seeking greatness discourage you from yours. Life goes on.

You should always remember that whatever your greatness is, do it with all that you have inside. Tomorrow is not promised; therefore, make a pivotal impact on the Earth while you are here alive in the flesh today. Leave a positive legacy for future generations. Be known as a survivor because life goes on.

Even If You're Getting High

The time is now for you to make a change for the better. Even if you are addicted to something, it does not matter how far gone you think you are. You can make an awesome comeback. Be willing to work hard as you rise up to greatness, Jesus is with you, and He will see you through. No hard work goes un-noticed by Him. *1 Corinthians 15:58...* Every piece of the hard work that you do benefits you, contrary to whatever the devil may be telling you. Remember, the devil attacks the mind, so think in your heart good things about yourself.

Suppress just sitting there thinking and talking about your greatness. Start doing something right now, to ensure your success. Never wait until tomorrow or next week because tomorrow is not promised. *Proverbs 27:1... James 4:13-15...* Transform your dreams into reality. Right now, get up and start your path to greatness. Trust in the process. Stop putting off your dreams until everything is perfect.

You are uniquely and wonderfully made by God. *Psalm 139:14...* There is no one else like you. Your family needs you. The world needs you and your expertise. Your life is extremely valuable to everyone. We all have a purpose in this life. What is yours? Do not just live for yourself, live for others and allow your greatness to benefit the world. Put others first in front of yourself. Then, the Lord will open up doors beyond your belief.

Stop making excuses because excuses do not require any action. It is better to do something than nothing at all. People may say this as an excuse not to be great: "Well, if I only had this or that." "I am going to start on my greatness after I stop smoking this or that." "Who knows how long greatness will take?" "Maybe when I stop drinking so much, I will start on my dreams." "Maybe I will start being great after I get my life together, and get off of these drugs..." No! Get up, and move directly towards a change now. Start your path to greatness right now!

The stakes are too high to wait until tomorrow. You have been thinking and contemplating about your dreams long enough. It is time to apply action to your dreams and goals now! If you want it, then you should have it, and do not take no for an answer. Be an overachiever in the midst of chaos. Overcome any obstacle placed in front of you. _**Psalm 23:1-6...**_ _**1 John 2:12-14...**_ Even if you are getting high, never hesitate to try your best. God loves you, regardless of whatever was done. You are forgiven! _**Hebrews 8:12...**_ His love will never leave you. _**Romans 8:38-39...**_ _**2 Corinthians 2:10-11...**_

You are already great, so display it. Do not wait until the future. Do it now. From this day forward, make every day the best day of your life. No drug ever created will be able to keep you away from your promise.

Chapter Five

Perfect Peace

On Your Way to Greatness

Heavy Hearted

Heavy-hearted… Brokenhearted… ***Psalm 34:18… Psalm 102:1… Isaiah 61:1… Luke 4:18…*** Sometimes you may not know how you are going to get by, maybe not even knowing how you are going to make it through the night. You may be wondering why does bad things happen to you. Or, why do you have to feel so much pain? Then in your darkest hour, the very people who were by your side before, have suddenly disappeared.

The heart is not just what keeps you alive. Your heart also is who you are as a person. ***1 Samuel 16:7…*** Eventually, what is in your heart will come out of you. Your positive outcome in life will depend on what is in your heart. Follow your dreams and purpose in life through the mighty heart. Let whatever puts joy in your heart be the guidance system for your purpose.

Your purpose in life has to mean more than silver and gold. A strategy to identify your purpose in life is to ask yourself, "What can I do for the world that would be spiritually healthy for humanity?" Ask yourself, "What gift can I provide in a positive way to serve humanity?" When your purpose becomes an obsession it will pull you through the tough challenges and give you the confidence to rise above life circumstances. Allow the mighty heart to direct you to your purpose and down the path into the light.

Studies have found that there is a very powerful field of energy surrounding the heart. This has been proven on a quantum-physics level. According to www.healingheartpower.com, "The magnetic field produced by the heart is five thousand times greater in strength than the field generated by the brain. The electromagnetic energy of the heart not only envelops every cell of the human body, but also extends out in all directions in the space around us." Electromagnetic energy from the heart extends into infinity. The heart also receives intuitive information before the brain does.

According to www.healingheartpower.com, "The heart is the first organ to form in the body. It is the organizing factor for physical formation, including the brain. The heart instantaneously communicates electromagnetic and chemical information to the rest of the body and to other bodies near it." The heart is more rational than the brain.

According to the Heart Math Institute, the heart possesses a level of intelligence that Heart Science is only beginning to understand. Science has proven that the heart has about 40,000 neurons that can sense, feel, and remember. The heart has its own intelligence, separate from the brain. Humans can only use a very small portion of their brains, but they can use their whole entire heart. Always ask the heart for answers.

You may say, "If the heart is so intuitive and smart, how does it get broken so easily?" The answer is, the heart actually gets stronger from adversity and pain. Open your heart and fill it with the love of Jesus. If you fill it with the world, this world's pain will crush you and your purpose completely. Let Jesus be your heart.

No one or anything on Earth can satisfy your desire to be loved. It has to be the love of Jesus that covers your heart. **_Proverbs 4:23..._** A heavy or broken heart is when a human being suffers from emotional or physical loss. There is a medical condition called, "The Broken Heart Syndrome". The Broken Heart Syndrome is a condition in which heart muscles are weakened temporarily. Symptoms includes, chest pains or shortness of breath.

A broken heart can only do two things for you. It can make you feel sorry for yourself and say, "Why me?" "Poor me..." and lose the fight, or it can ignite you to trust totally in Jesus to see you through. Practice on controlling your emotions. Stay calm and at rest. Get out of your mind and listen to your heart. This is how you win the fight. Do not let the ego put the mind and the heart at war. Synchronize the two and make them one in Christ consciousness. You cannot rush this process of synchronization because it requires training. You train by immersing yourself in God's Word.

Greatness comes through pain and adversity, so you cannot be afraid of it. Conquer it. It is totally because of Christ you can say that you are a conqueror. Jesus cares about every part of your heart. You have the power to make it through anything, especially a troubled heart. Trust the Lamb, He has your heart protected. Jesus will take the weight off of your heavy heart.

The Champion In You

There is an undying champion in each one of you. Why? Because Jesus is the "Sinless Champion". *2 Corinthians 5:21...* He has not ever lost a match and never will. He is undisputed! Never let the world extinguish your belief in you. You cannot let the enemy rob you of your identity. You are a champion.

Why are you a champion, you may ask? You are a champion, because Jesus Christ rose from the dead with all power in his hands. *Mark 16:1...* You are operating on the finished works of Christ. In the Greek the finished works or saved is known as "Sozo". "Sozo" is a Greek word that means healed, saved, and delivered. "Sozo" also means to save from destruction or to restore to completeness.

With Sozo, you can walk in the Spirit and purpose for which you have been called. For example, Sozo is the inexhaustible personal bodyguard for you. Sozo deflects every shot that the devil shoots at you. Sozo gets in the way or intervenes on anything hindering you from your "Perfect Peace". In life there will be many challenges in front of you, but victory will be worth the challenge in the end. "Manasseh," God will make you forget your affliction. *Genesis 41:51...* Manasseh is an ancient Hebrew language name for men meaning "causing to forget".

In Christ, even your losses are wins because your losses will lead you to your promise. The blood has completely released you from failure. *Hebrews 13:20...* You just have to believe it and have a pro-longed patience. *Hebrews 6:11-12...* Never underestimate the heart of a champion. Faith in the finished works of Jesus makes you a "faith champion". *Hebrews 4:1-3 NIV...*

Be confident and do not be afraid to show your greatness. You are a champion. Pray like it! Act like it! Talk like it! Walk like it! Look like it! Smell like it! There is no time not to live like a champion. There is no time to feel defeated. A champion is thinking about winning the entire time. A champion always plays the game of life with heart and passion. Jesus paid it all for you to be a champion. Use the powers and gifts that He has supplied through His blood. Follow Jesus so the real champion in you can be displayed.

Hopeless?

Hopeless? Hopeless is a word for the defeated. No one can be hopeless in Christ Jesus. Many people that have the feeling of hopelessness or depression contemplate on committing suicide. Please, don't do it. You are exponentially loved! About every 40 seconds, someone chooses to end his or her own life. Hopelessness and depression are responsible for at least half of the suicides worldwide. Millionaires with "everything" are committing suicides as well. So, it is not money and wealth that make a person happy.

Long ago, in the savage or primitive world, suicides were unheard of. But in this so-called advanced, civilized world, suicides are rampant and are increasing. It makes you wonder, which civilization is, or was, really primitive? The advanced civilization may have the technology, but they do not have the happiness the primitive people had. The primitive people were very closely knit to their family and friends. They were not competing to see who could buy the most expensive cell phone.

Actually the Earth is considered a type-zero civilization and has a long way to go according to the Kardashev scale. The Kardashev scale is a method of measuring a civilization's level of technology advancement, based on the amount of energy a civilization is able to utilize directed towards communication. The scale has three designated categories called Type-one, two, and three.

The inhabitants on Earth still harness their needs from dead plants and animals, which is known as fossil fuels. A type-one civilization can harness all of their energy from a neighboring star. Harnessing energy from a neighboring star would allow the Earth to meet and store energy needs for everyone easily.

Type-two civilizations and beyond can achieve some astronomical feats that we are far away from achieving. But, it is not impossible for humanity on Earth to achieve these awesome feats. Humanity must work together to extinguish war and allow advanced scientific discoveries to flourish. Nothing is ever impossible or hopeless.

Hopelessness and depression can arise from many factors. The brain is an awesome tool when used properly. The brain is absolutely miraculous and needs to be taken seriously. Brain study is vital and should be a curriculum in the school system. Brain study could save scores of lives and would begin to suppress hopelessness and depression.

An interesting study has been done on babies that are still in their mother's womb. The studies have found that a fetus can be greatly affected by the outside environment. The fetus tries to make sense or perceive what type of world it is about to enter. Situations could have happened in the past that are deeply embedded in the brain of the unborn baby.

A positive or negative environment affects the baby in the womb. Therefore, a negative environment can result in the offspring having emotional distress and feelings within their bodies that they cannot explain, especially when the person becomes an adult. The doctor may just prescribe some anxiety pills to the patient because it is more profitable to write prescriptions, resulting in never getting to the root of the problem.

Somebody may have been raped or abandoned in the past. Maybe someone reading this has been abused physically, emotionally, or mentally. Or there could just be a number of issues going on within the body that the individual cannot explain. Those feelings can be very frustrating, but it is not hopeless. There could be an "epigenetic" affect going on. Epigenetic means "relating to or arising from non-genetic influences on gene expression." Therefore, that means a person's environment means a tremendous amount.

There could be some negative events that happened in the past, situations that the individual cannot even remember. This process is called "implicit memory" in the brain. A person's environment could have greatly affected them while they were still in the womb. Situations could have happened to the unborn baby before their brain was fully developed. That is why some people have certain feelings within the body that they cannot explain. It is like a file downloaded into the brain waiting for some experience to trigger it. In many cases, this can lead to the feeling of hopelessness or depression.

"Explicit memory" is the opposite of "implicit memory". Explicit memory relates to the events that are remembered in the brain from past or present situations. Negative, uncontrollable situations in the past or present can trigger depression. These studies can be used as a tool to recognize and understand some functions within the brain. Knowing how the brain works can help someone conquer hopelessness and depression. Ninety-five percent of an individual's behavior is controlled by subconscious beliefs, beliefs that the environment demonstrated to the individual.

Eighty percent of subconscious thoughts are negative. The hopeless mind repeats the same defeated thoughts perpetually. Negative thoughts affect every cell within the body, although new neurons in the brain can be created when negative acts are broken. It is extremely important not to live in your mind and make it your identity. Think with your heart when negative thoughts or feelings surface. Your heart will always choose to love. The goal is to become an all positive individual. **_Matthew 5:48..._** The brain is a wonderful tool, but it is not who the individual is as a person.

If something was done to you in the past, you may not understand why. But let it go in your heart. Empty your heart and fill it with love and compassion. Do not cover up the unwanted feelings that you have inside. Allow yourself to let go and feel them. This will begin your forgiving and healing process because you cannot heal what you do not feel. Forgiveness is one of God's greatest creations.

You cannot control someone else's unconscious actions. It is not your fault if something was done to you, and you are far from being a failure. Maybe you are a person that has hurt someone in the past. You must forgive yourself to heal. Peace will only come about when you forgive yourself. You are a new person now. Your old hurtful ways has transformed into blessing ways. Christ consciousness protects you from past, present, and future pains.

Christ, the tender-hearted, protects His sheep from all emotional pains, even emotional pains that they cannot explain within their bodies. Jesus will take all of the pain away. Just ask Him for help. He is your hope out of depression. Furthermore, a positive, loving environment for an individual is essential and lifesaving.

Choose life is the Word of God. Wouldn't you rather live life on God's terms, and not yours? ***Deuteronomy 30:15-20...*** Emotional pain within the body needs fuel to survive. It derives its strength from past and present situations which have not been dealt with. Your past and present situations are just life circumstances. Living in the past does not make you who you are. Being great at this very moment does. Jesus offers greatness at this very moment. You can do anything. ***Luke 1:37...*** You can live your life abundantly. ***John 10:10...*** Maybe there are some bad things surrounding you in your life, and you may feel like your walls are closing in on you. The things that are going on right now are just a test of your faith. Have faith in the fog, and the Lord will be your guiding light.

You have to believe that your current situation is not the finished product. Always continue to evolve. There is a better you right ahead. Allow the past situations and bad decisions in your life to pass away. ***Proverbs 4:25...*** It is time to invent the new you now. All of the events that happened in the past has led you to this very moment of spiritual awareness. It does not matter how many mistakes were made in the past. You are full of hope. The light inside of you will light up. You cannot rush the light. It takes a person that has been in the dark to gradually see the light.

Never allow your mind to control you and become cloudy. Filter those foul things out of your mind. You control the mind. _**1 Peter 1:13...**_ Do not let it control you. That is just like a car or computer controlling you. Use your mind as a wonderful tool and not as an adversary. Stop thinking negatively or over-thinking matters. Drop it! Always have hope. Invent the new you that will not ever give up or quit, the new you that's a fighter to the very end!

Hopeless? It is never hopeless. You are destined for greatness no matter what! Your mind is a very powerful weapon. Never use it against yourself. What you think about yourself and say determines what you ultimately become. Never talk badly about yourself because your body "hears" you, and that will only put you in a corner of despair. Despair leads to the road of hopelessness. You are unique and special with varied talents at your disposal. God put you upon the Earth for a distinct purpose. Life is very beautiful with Jesus Christ from Nazareth. Try Him when the feeling of hopelessness or depression sets in. Killing yourself is not the answer. Your whole Christian family all around the world loves you. Your Christian family embraces you. Always choose life.

Screaming to God is not necessary, He can hear you. _**Psalm 34:17...**_ God is already with you and hears your cry for help. _**Isaiah 49:15-16...**_ Never let your situation dictate who you are or what you start to believe. Those situations are only temporary. It is never hopeless. Always think like a winner in any predicament. Do not worry about what you see right now. God has not changed His mind about you. You are still on the list for deliverance.

You are just one play away from going all of the way. There is always an unlimited amount of hope, especially when you know who you are in Christ. Be confident in yourself. You are an image of Christ. You are bursting at the seams, full of hope!

Knowing Whose You Are

God put thought into creating you. You are irreplaceable. **_Psalm 139:14..._** Everything in life is not going to be all copacetic. There are still valuable life lessons that need to be learned and experienced to further your growth. There are going to be many obstacles and hurdles to conquer. "Only the strong will survive." Only the strong in the mind will survive.

Keep your spirits high and stay on fire for the Lord. Remember who you are when the devil is upon you. The devil wants you to question the Lord and make you feel worthless or helpless. He relishes in your feeling like there is no way out. If you are sick, today will be the last day that you will say you are sick. Do not just depend on what the doctor says. Instead, consult with God and give Him the last word. Always ask God for direction. He has healed individuals through grace with the rarest diseases.

God works through you by faith. Through the blood you are healed. You just have to choose which one that you want. Who can heal your body? Who can make you whole? Nobody but Jesus! **_Mark 1:40-45..._** **_Mark 5:1-20..._** Jesus has supplied healing on the cross. He gave you the power to be healed every day, no matter what you see or feel. **_Luke 9:1-2..._** Praise and confidence in God totally confuses the enemy. Say that you are healed.

Say, "I am healed right now by Christ's stripes. Pain and sickness, you must go." Say that with authority over and over again. Chant it! You are in control, not the sickness or ailment. Never say again that you are sick. Say instead, "I'm healed." **_Matthew 10:1-8..._** Be a survivor and give that medical condition all that you have. Remember whose you are. You must call out things that are not as though they were! **_Romans 4:17..._**

You have to control your tongue. A quick blurt out of your own words and thinking can ruin everything. **_Proverbs 13:3..._** Let the Word of God be your supernatural medicine. **_Isaiah 53:5..._** There is nothing like God's medicine because there is not anything like the blood of the Lamb. The devil is a liar, and the truth is nowhere in him. **_John 8:44..._** Have the faith of a mustard seed, and you will be healed. You may not feel well right now or the next day, but never say it. Have patience. You must develop a sustained faith and not a sporadic one. **_Hebrews 10:36..._** Sometimes you have to chip away at the pain, and sometimes the pain vanishes on demand.

Always say, "All is well with you," even if you do not see it at the time. Keep on attacking that sickness with your supernatural medicine. The more you use your supernatural medicine, the stronger you will become. There are some no-medicine hospitals in various cultures around the world. The patient at the no-medicine hospital receives healing through eating correctly, prayer, and most of all, faith! Huge tumors have disappeared in minutes with faith as the only medicine.

Science has proven that prayer is very beneficial to an ailing patient. The patient that prayed, and was prayed for by others had a much better outcome than the patient that did not. The way to get your prayers answered is to believe, and live your life as if your prayer has already been answered. Live as if you are healed already. Your relief is coming soon. God's timing is impeccable. Impeccable timing is what makes His miracles so spectacular. **_Luke 9:12-17..._**

Praising God completely fools the enemy. You will be claiming victory in the face of despair. **_1 Corinthians 15:57..._** You may say, "I still feel down and depressed after I do all of that." The reason why you are still feeling depressed is because you are still holding on to the supposed failure or problem. Do not attach yourself to the supposed sickness or ailment. Let it go. You cannot let it torment you in the mind. Remember who you are.

Perpetual thinking and worrying can actually bring about a sickness. Not forgiving yourself or other people can cause sicknesses as well. The sickness comes about because the body wants you to stop stressing. The body shuts down when it is over stressed. It is the body's way to slow you down. It is not wise to work and worry yourself into a sickness when peace and tranquility is available abundantly.

God has a plan that will set you free of any despair or illness. If any man or woman be in Jesus, He will take the pain away. *2 Corinthians 5:17...* The Word of God will alleviate any pain or anxiety that you feel. You just have to know whose you are. Not knowing whose you are will have you doing things on your own. Listen to the Holy Spirit. Follow the Lamb, He will give you a "Crown of Life". *James 1:12...* He is the King of Peace that sits upon the throne. *Revelation 4:9-11...*

If you start to feel over stressed, calm down and take a few deep breaths. Place your hand over your heart. Breathe in five seconds, and release five seconds. Feel the blood rush and heartbeat in your body. You are fully alive, are you not? Trust in Christ, the Savior, because after all, He is the only one that will be in that pine box with you at the end. He is the Judge! *John 8:36... John 14:6... Matthew 25:31-46... 2 Corinthians 5:10...* Furthermore, never let anyone or anything steal your joy. All sickness or distractions must go. Perfect Peace belongs to you. Don't you know who you are?

Nobody or anything can stand in your way when you know whose you are. It is like creating your own universe in your mind, your own world, just you and Christ. *John 16:33... 1 John 5:4-5...* Some people will distract you from remembering whose you are because they have not yet become Christ conscious. Continue to live in "Perfect Peace" through Christ and allow people to see the light through you. *John 12:46...* Darkness cannot survive in the light. *John 1:5...*

Christians do not have to react. Christians relax; True Christians rest because Christians know who they are. Jesus said, "He will give you the desires of your heart." *Psalm 37:4...* Desire His heavenly blessings and peace and not the world's pain. You are already healed. You are already released from anxiety and stress. Christ has already gone before you in your journey. He has already been here at this very moment. He conquered time and knows your future, so that means you are protected through and through. You are protected from the front, back, and sides.

Whatever you ask in Jesus's name will be supplied to you. ***John 14:13-14...*** You just have to believe it and remember whose you are. Terminate worrying about anything. Take everything to the Lord in prayer. ***Philippians 4:6... Romans 10:13...*** Remember, He is the Judge. ***2 Corinthians 5:9-10...*** So just relax and rest your nerves. Be glad. Neither sickness nor any other creature shall be able to stand against your peace. You are the child of "The Holy King". That is who you are.

Be One In Christ

"For unto us a Child is born, unto us a Son was given: and the government shall be upon his shoulders: and His name will be called, Wonderful, Counselor, mighty God, The Everlasting Father, and The Prince of Peace" (**Isaiah 9:6 KJV).** This powerful scripture was prophesied by Isaiah 700 years before Christ was born. **_John 12:41..._**

Be one in Christ. "Make two into one, and the inside like the outside, and the outside like the inside." In Christ you will become a demigod or demigoddess. He will give you His power. A demigod can do all things because their God can do all things. A demigod? Yes. It is as if you take a drop of water out of the Pacific Ocean. That drop of water has all of the composition of the big body of water. Symbolically, you are that drop of water. You have all of the composition of God. Christians are one in Him.

Be careful, do not allow the ego to take over and believe that you **_are_** God. You are an extension of Him. Christians are congruent with Him. **_John 17:21..._** **_Romans 12:4-5..._** God gives His followers assignments to perform on His behalf. With God, your power is unlimited. A human life has no value when it is cut off from God. For example, if you cut a limb off of your body and throw it into the street, the limb automatically becomes worthless. But when it was connected to the body, the limb was priceless. A person's life is worthless when it is cut off from God.

It is essential to never let down your guard. **_Colossians 3:2..._** The devil is lurking around, searching for a heart that has a disconnection from Christ, searching for a heart that is not trusting and believing. The enemy is looking for someone to torment in the mind and doubt themselves. The devil just loves it because he knows that a person that is not one in Christ will be an easy target, easy pickings for the enemy.

The devil will have unconnected people thinking and doing ludicrous things; for instance, shooting and killing their own neighbor. Youth are talking back and disrespecting their parents. *2 Timothy 3:2-7...* That is why so many of the youth are dying in droves today. Children must obey their parents to live a long, prosperous life upon the Earth. *Ephesians 6:1-3... Colossians 3:20...* Millions of prostitutes are walking the streets making money for sex. All kinds of evil exist because of this disconnection. One minute without Christ can cost you your life or sanity. Stay in Him at all times! Be one in Him.

You may ask, "How do I know when there is a disconnection?" You will know when your happiness starts to fade. You will also know when your stress levels begin to increase heavily. You will become easily irritated and start to judge. Your mind will become extremely cloudy and start to over-think things. Stay connected to Him. Be one in Him.

The pre-cross era is the era of history before Christ sacrificed His life on the cross. Humanity must end living life in the pre-cross era. People who live and think in the pre-cross era are still living with the traditions of the old. They are still living with old customs and beliefs. *Galatians 1:6-10... Colossians 2:20-23...* There was an inestimable amount of history before Jesus came upon the Earth. Those old traditions and customs are still relevant to history. But after the cross, it was finished! *John 19:30...* Jesus was appointed by God to save the whole Earth at a specific time in history. *Isaiah 7:14... Isaiah 11:1-10... Micah 5:2... Psalm 22:16...*

John the Baptist was sent by God to bear witness about the "Light" (Jesus Christ). John the Baptist's purpose in life was to spread the gospel of *grace* and to recognize the coming of the Savior. There is a story in the Bible about when John the Baptist saw Jesus in Bethany across the Jordan River, where John was baptizing believers. *John 1:28...* When John the Baptist saw Jesus coming toward him, he said, "Behold, the Lamb of God, who takes away the sins of the world!" *John 1:29...*

John the Baptist knew that there were many imposters that had come to the Earth before who claimed to be Christ. *__Luke 17:22-25...__* *__Matthew 24:23-27...__* But, God Almighty gave John the Baptist specific signs to indicate the *only* coming of Christ. The rest of the presumed gods in history were only shadows or depictions of the real thing.

John gave this testimony, "I saw the Spirit come down from the heaven as a dove and remain on him. And I myself did not know him, but the one who sent me to baptize with water told me, 'The man on whom you see the Spirit come down and remain is the one who will baptize with the Holy Spirit.' I have seen and testify that this is God's Chosen One" (*John 1:32-34 NIV*).

God sent Jesus as a sacrifice "once" and for "all". *__Hebrews 10:10-14...__* All other sacrifices were to cease. Sin was the problem before the cross. Humanity was believing in false gods and saviors, which still persist in today's society. After the cross, Christ made His sheep perfect. *__Matthew 5:48...__* Jesus wiped *all* sin away. Jesus received all of the sins of this world on the cross, and His sheep received God's righteousness. He handled it. Remember, the miracle is in God's timing. Jesus was a gift from God! Grace was supplied abundantly after the cross. *__1 Corinthians 15:55-57...__* Live a graced life, and be one in Him.

Christ's sheep hear His voice and know Him by name. *__John 10:14-30...__* If you are a person who has not heard His voice, it is probably because you are not listening. Whatever you need, He has it. *__Philippians 4:19...__* *__John 14:12-14...__* Everyone will make mistakes in life, but you are always on the right side with Jesus. Satan and his demons are in collusion to destroy or sear your good conscience. *__1 Timothy 4:1-2...__* *__1 Timothy 1:18-19...__* *__Titus 1:15...__* Satan and his demons are at every vantage point looking for weak-minded individuals.

Let the Word of God enter into your heart to reside so that Satan will not be able to snatch away what has been sown. *__Luke 8:12-15...__* *__Matthew 13:19...__* The devil is always trying to catch someone disconnected from Christ. But nothing can separate you from the love of God when you let Him be your heart. So be one in Him. *__Romans 8:38...__*

Whatcha Looking For?

Many people are looking for something or someone to fulfill them, something to make them feel validated in life. There are millions of people that are stressed out and in unwavering pain. Bill collectors are calling relentlessly. Warrants are piling up, and nerves are all bad over things that have taken place in the past. Some people are just wondering how they are going to make it through the day. You may say that no one understands your situation, or that your situation is hopeless. *1 Peter 5:9...* You may think nothing will ever change.

Tremendous pain is saturating the world. A perpetuation of evil permeates throughout generations. You may wonder, who can get you out of these disasters? I have great news today and forevermore. I know a man that can change your night into day. At your darkest hour is when He shines the most. That man's name is Jesus Christ! *Acts 16:25-26...* There is no one like Him, nor will there ever be. *Jude 1:25...*

Many may ask, "How do I connect myself with this great Jesus?" First of all, just call upon His Holy name. *Romans 10:11-13...* Then, you will have to start looking for Him instead of searching for outside forces to make you happy. You will have to seek the Kingdom of the Lord. Put Him first above all things. *Matthew 6:23... Matthew 6:31...* The battle is in your conscience. *Peter 4:1... 1 Corinthians 2:16...* What you think about yourself needs to be based upon the Word and not the world.

Jesus is always on the scene, and He is extraordinarily in love with you! He is right by your side at all times. Look for Him in all situations. He is the love you have been searching for the whole time. His love will never die. There is no way that it can.

People will surely disappoint you. They will not ever look at you the way that Jesus does. Material and physical things will fade away, but Jesus will remain forever. What are you looking for? Christ's love has been right there with you the entire time.

Chapter Six

Perfect Peace

On Your Way to Greatness

Live in the Supernatural Realm

Supernatural: Events in which the forces of nature or man cannot produce. Supernatural is a divine operation that transcends what is normal and cannot be explained. The supernatural realm defies all laws of physics and surpasses worldly mind comprehension. Every bit of the world says that it is impossible to be supernatural. You must think and dwell in the supernatural realm to see supernatural results. Never doubt the unique state of the supernatural mind regardless of what the world may say.

Humans are distinctly different from every species that has ever been created on this Earth, so do not think carnally. A carnal-minded person is as close to an animal as a human can get, so think the impossible. **_2 Corinthians 10:4..._** Even the Angels are not able to have the same relationship with God as humans. **_Psalm 8:5..._** We are a very privileged species. Humanity can have a one-on-one relationship with the Creator, and He made us in His own image. **_Genesis 1:27..._** Therefore, that means you are more than just mere flesh and blood. You can kiss the face of God through your worship.

The comprehension of God is what separates mankind from animals. Humans have the ability to know and understand God. Plants and animals do not. You are a supernatural being with an eternal soul. You can do some amazing things with your life. You can do things that look like miracles to other people. Humanity cannot trust in science and history to prove God's existence because science and history are still trying to catch up with the Word. Science and history are remarkable tools for obtaining knowledge, but science and history discredited events in the

Word. Those same discredited events are all coming into the light now.

Most scientists know that there is a God. **_Romans 1:21-32..._** They are just trying to explain His supernatural miracles. Would you search for something that you knew was not in existence at all? There is a particular particle called the God particle, for which scientists are searching. This particle is also known as the "Higgs boson". The scientists at CERN smash sub-atomic particles together, almost at the speed of light. It is said that CERN may be experimenting with opening up wormholes or stargates. The scientists use a Large Hadron Collider to smash these particles together.

The Large Hadron Collider is the largest single machine in the world. The so-called God particle is supposed to explain how the universe was created. The world may be waiting a while for that. CERN will need a much bigger machine to figure out God. No man-made machine will be able to reach God. It is the spiritual or supernatural that reaches God, not machines. It takes a pure heart to dwell with God. "Blessed are the pure in heart, for they will see God" *(Matthew 5:8 NIV)*. **_Psalm 24:4-5..._**

There is absolutely nothing wrong with trying to understand God. The calamity occurs when mankind starts to believe that they *are* God. Trust the Word and not man. Some things just cannot be explained until it is time to be revealed. For instance, how did God form the world with words? Or how does something invisible like air keep us alive? We cannot see the air, but it is what's flowing through our lungs, keeping us alive. We cannot see God, but He is the one keeping us all alive. It is the unseen that is most important. The Supernatural! Tread the unknown. Step out of the boat. Do not believe in only what you can see and touch. That is carnal thinking. You cannot physically see someone's thoughts, but you know they are thinking something.

"Get rich or die trying" is an insane way of thinking. It has mammon and unrest written all over it. Money and riches are only an illusion. Money is completely worthless. It was created out of nothing. It is just paper that man made. The banks create money out of thin air then tax the poor for the money that they just made up. Isn't it insane to kill someone over paper? For the love of money is the root of all evil. *1 Timothy 6:10...* The system is set up for people to fight, steal, and do other wild things for money. The scarcity or greed of money is why most crimes occur.

Money creates a slave out of the person who loves it. A money slave can never rest. The slave mind always hears the cracking of the master's whip in the background. Sometimes it seems as if the devil has put a cloak or a block on the brains of people so they will not think supernaturally. *2 Corinthians 4:4...* They will only believe in what the world tells them. We live in a world where only money matters. If it does not develop a profit, it is worthless in this world. There are many geniuses in the world with an invention sitting on the shelf because it may not generate mass profits, or the invention would put some big billion-dollar company out of business. People are sick, hungry, and homeless today because of greed.

Diseases has killed more people than a terrorists ever have. However, billions of dollars are funded for a war against terror. If those billions were concentrated for medical research and cures instead of a senseless war, millions of people would be cured of their terrible diseases, not to mention that all hunger on Earth would be eradicated. Every five seconds a child dies from malnutrition and hunger, not every five minutes. Every five seconds! This is the civilized world, right? Maybe history will look back and see that this generation was not so civilized at all. This generation puts material goods before their own neighbors' needs.

Profit and greed are everything in this world, and living in the supernatural realm is not. This world needs a heavy dose of love and spiritual integrity. A love warrior would put their life and reputation on the line to fight for truth, justice, honesty, and decency. A love warrior lives in the supernatural realm.

Humanity must be aware and avoid the traps of the government and thriving medical field. The apathetic government and medical market cannot afford for people to be aware, healed, healthy, and vibrant, because that would result in a loss of profit. If everyone were healthy, the people in the government and bustling medical field would not be able to afford their luxurious lifestyles. In this cruel, greedy world, profit and senseless war come before a human life. This is not saying that there are not any good doctors. There are many great doctors that are changing and saving lives every day. Great doctors help cure diseases and lives simultaneously.

A patient should not be a number, but they should be treated like someone's grandparent, mother, father, or child. Great doctors do the job for the love of serving humanity. Over 200,000 people per year die from medical malpractice. According to www.naturalnews.com, iatrogenesis is America's number three killer. Iatrogenesis means "any injury or illness because of medical care." A doctor that takes lives through malpractice and for money does not live in the supernatural realm.

There are doctors that are participating in the inhumane process of Eugenics. Eugenics is the science of improving a human population by controlled breeding to increase the occurrence of desirable heritable characteristics. According to Eugenics News, studies have found that vaccines can be used to target a certain race. A convert depopulation program is being run by the World Health Organization targeting Africans for extermination via infertility chemicals administered under the guise of "vaccines". These malicious practices are wiping out the people of color upon the Earth.

Poisoned water has been found in the lower-income communities. Heavy traces of lead in water supplies have been found in the Hispanic, African American, and Native American communities. Heavy doses of lead cause cancer and other numerous negative effects within the body. Vitamin D blocks cancer, but this information was not relayed to the community. Vitamin D kills cancer cells within the human body.

Vitamin B-17 or Laetrile can be used to eradicate cancer as well. Vitamin B-17 is derived from the kernels of apricot pits. Shouldn't this life-saving information be reported in the mainstream media? This should make you ponder who really has your best interest in mind? The mainstream media is saturated with scare tactics, engineered diseases, government shut downs, scandals, and greedy apathetic politicians. Humanity should be wondering how many more life-saving cures and information is being withheld from the public.

In some known instances, the medical market has injected diseases in their medicine and supplied it to the public for money. They cause the problem, then sell the cure. Vaccines, psychiatric medications, and various other pharmaceutical drugs have innumerous amounts of side effects. Cancer and infertility is on the rise in minority communities. The people in the minority community are being exterminated as if they were weeds. Congress and the federal government gave these bustling pharmaceutical companies complete immunity because if they were sued, the whole medical field would go bankrupt.

The media will not report this Holocaust cast upon the minorities. The disease-control companies are in control of the media. The news companies have to do as they are told. The disease-control companies and the media only create panic so they can continue to systematically poison the public. Autism, cancer, and infertility are only a few ways to weaken and depopulate people of color.

Via abortion, blacks are essentially being exterminated systematically, as statistics demonstrate: Not only abortion is dominant in the black communities, but for every black baby born, **three** are killed via the procedure according to Eugenics News. Abortion centers are predominantly set up in areas of cities where blacks are the majority demographic.

"The Planned Parenthood/abortion industry needs a steady supply of black women getting pregnant and wanting to terminate their pregnancy in order for them to be able to harvest [fetal] tissue and organs via partial-birth abortions, which are almost all black babies," according to Natural News founder Mike Adams. Many of these baby body parts are being sold for a profit. The Center for Medical Progress proved this via a series of released videos.

Satan uses abortion to kill off souls that would have come to Christ. Killing off the souls that would have come to Christ will only delay his upcoming demise. There are many more satanic traps set up for the minorities and the rest of humanity. Everyone on this planet is affected by disease-injected medicines and medical malpractices. That is why a doctor cannot be trusted *only* for your healing, but Jesus, the healer, can. He is the "Master Physician". He can, and will, handle it! It is absolutely necessary to live supernaturally because it can cost you your life.

Drug addiction is not the only addiction that plagues the Earth. For instance, society is addicted to money, fame, power, sex, various entertainments, war, etc. Tobacco kills at least five million people each year. Worldwide, alcohol kills a few million people per year. Worldwide, 570,000 people die from illegal drug use per year. Drug use has a drastically lower death rate than the big billion-dollar companies in the world.

But apathetic industries like the alcohol or tobacco companies will get a big bonus check and picture on the front of a magazine. These millionaires and billionaires are also getting paid from how many people get thrown in prison. Shouldn't the owner of the alcohol company be placed in prison for killing millions of people per year? Shouldn't the owner of the tobacco company be placed in prison for killing five million people per year, instead of the person that got caught with five dollars' worth of marijuana?

It is more profitable to put people in prison instead of helping them. Criminal-justice reform is long overdue! The alcohol and tobacco companies are committing murder. The individual that is addicted to drugs or alcohol has a disorder. These individuals should be helped, not thrown in prison.

The higher the stock market or GDP numbers are in the world, the higher prison rates, death rates, homicides, poverty, hunger, and mental illnesses will be increased with it. Where is all of the money going? The money is certainly not going to the hungry, homeless, or sick. The GDP is also a measure for the destruction of natural wealth. The higher the GDP or stock market, the more forests, jungles, rivers and fresh water around the planet are being destroyed.

The richest one percent has more wealth than the rest of the world combined. If you have food, clothes, and a roof over your head; you are better off than 83% of the people on the planet. The system is set up for the rich to stay rich and the poor to stay poor. That is why the rich are given all of the big tax breaks, bailouts, and bonuses. *James 5:1-6...* The socioeconomic gradient is real. This world can be very unequal, unethical, and fraudulent.

The indifference to evil and inequality is heinous in itself. Justice and love must be indivisible. Fortunately, those evil traps of the enemy will not work on a supernatural being. A supernatural being is already rich. A supernatural being is already healed. So when a doctor comes with a diagnosis that cannot be cured, tell them, "It is a good thing that I am already healed in Jesus's name." Say, "I know that He already worked it out!" A supernatural being already know that their Lord will come through and heal any incurable disease by *faith*. Remember, Jesus resurrected Lazarus from the dead. *John 11:38-43...*

Jesus said, "And I will do whatever you ask in my name, so that the Father may be glorified in the Son. You may ask me anything in my name, and I will do it" *(John 14:13-14 NIV).* A supernatural mind will give you the sense to visualize the enemy clearly. When you are in your supernatural mind, the enemy has no chance. The enemy is anyone or anything hindering you from "Perfect Peace".

Craving material items only takes your mind away from the supernatural realm. Everything that you purchase is designed to fail or malfunction; for example, your phone, car, computer, television and tires, etc. All of these products can be designed to the best of their ability and not to fail. But again, that would result in a loss of profit. Abundance and efficient innovation are the enemy of the world. The system needs you to be a slave and crave worthless items. *Proverbs 22:7...* The system feeds on retail therapy. Material things will not fulfill a heart, only love will.

According to CBSnews.com, a handful of conglomerates are selling handbags marked up by as much as 20 times what they cost to make. Designer fashion sells for a whopping 12 times the cost to make. The television constantly advertises and programs people's minds to desire worthless material items. The television and advertisement industry falsifies what life is really about, a false reality. The advertisement industry wants to control your neurons. They want to set your life value system for you. The system needs people to go right on along with their plan and not think about the supernatural realm.

It is essential not to conform to this world because before you know it, you may start to resemble or have the same exact desires of the world, and not think supernaturally. For example, materialism, narcissism, flaunting, fighting, aggression, jealousy, anxiety, stress, lusting for money, and just having complete hate for one another are distractions from the true enjoyment of a supernatural life. ***Titus 3:3...*** You are one with everything ever made. Bear the image of the heavenly man, the supernatural Savior. (Jesus) ***1 Corinthians 15:44-49...***

There was a research study once done on a couple of groups of chimpanzees. One group was placed where there was an abundance of everything they needed. The other group was placed where there was a scarcity of provisions.

The chimps with the abundance were shown sharing and caring for one another. They were all working together as one unit. But the chimps that were placed in lack were always at odds with each other. They were selfish and would even fight to the death! Their environment was never at peace. This is the same deranged system that has been set up for humanity. The system only exists because the people allow it.

People think it is normal to fight and compete for everything. The Earth is filled with an abundance of everything we will ever need. ***Genesis 1:1... Genesis 1:26...*** The Earth just cannot supply everyone's greed. The Earth was given to us by God. It was not supposed to be controlled by the government, giant companies, banks, or mammon. Every single need has already been supplied on the cross by the blood. Therefore, hate and envy are not ever necessary. **_1 Peter 2:1..._** You can do some amazing things with your supernatural mind because there is no limit to your potential.

Your supernatural mind separates you from this world and protects you from the pain of the enemy. All of the traps and clever tricks of the enemy will malfunction. This world's system will not affect a supernatural individual, because no weapon formed against them will ever prosper. A supernatural being will not conform, desire, or imitate this world. A supernatural being does not need material items to make them happy. God is all they need and desire.

Supernatural beings defeat the devil by spreading love and compassion. Supernatural beings ignite others to wake up and to stop following the devil into a meaningless life. So, do not ever live in the natural! Always live supernaturally where this world's pain, social inequalities, desires, scams, clever traps, and way of thinking is obsolete. Do great things with your life and achieve greatness. Live every day as if it was your last. Living in the natural puts limits on your entire life. Living in natural and carnal thinking puts limits on your greatness. Live supernaturally unceasingly.

If There's a Will, There's a Way

Sometimes, it may seem, no matter how hard you press and work, nothing is going the way that you want to. You try to lose weight, or you have been trying to find a job or lover. You may be wondering when you are going to get a big break. There are millions of possibilities of things that could be going wrong right now, but do not focus on them because that will only get you down and depressed. It is okay to strategize, but do not harp on your shortcomings or losses. *__Isaiah 61:7...__* All is well with you. *__2 Kings 4:26...__* Christ will restore triple fold whatever is lost. *__Deuteronomy 30:3...__*

Never be easily irritated or offended on your way to greatness. Stay persistent in the Word. Getting offended or wearing your feelings on your sleeve can make you completely miss out on your blessing. Have faith that Jesus will come through from anywhere or through any circumstance. Your faith will produce a straightway blessing, a sudden blessing because of your strong belief in Christ. *__Matthew 15:22-28...__*

All of your hard work is being counted by the Most High. Never think that your hard work and time is being wasted. *__1 Corinthians 10:31...__* It takes time and hard work to reach the top of the mountain. If greatness were easy, everyone would be at the top. Sometimes you will be uncomfortable on your way to success. Just know that God is working in the background. If there is a will, there is a way.

God goes before, with, and behind you in your journey to success. You are covered 360 degrees. *__Psalm 5:12...__* *__Psalm 23:6...__* He is always working behind the scenes on your behalf because it is not easy to be great. It is hard work. If you are sick or in the hospital, your condition right now is not going to last forever. It does not matter what type of disease it is. If it is even a disease at all? It could just be a test to see if you will use your supernatural abilities, your supernatural medicine. **_Psalm 34:17-20..._** Get your mind on Christ and His healing power. **_Hebrews 11:6..._** If there is a will, there is a way.

Pick your Bible up and hold it close to your heart, because by Jesus Christ's stripes you are healed. You have to believe and know that He is right there in the midst with you! **_Matthew 14:22-33..._** You are His sheep. His breath flows through your lungs. You have supernatural powers right within you. Your belief in your being healed right now is totally in your power. Jesus has given you the power within through amazing grace.

Be strong in the mind. Do not let what you see or feel right now determine your outcome. **_Matthew 14:31..._** You must confuse the enemy. Count it all joy! Praise in the midst of turmoil. Look danger right in the eye. If you are in jail or prison, conquer your fear. Keep praising God and turn the whole prison into a revival. You cannot be stopped! If Jesus is for you, who on Earth has the audacity to defeat or keep you away from your greatness? **_Romans 8:31..._** If there is a will, there is a way, because you know Jesus Christ Himself. **_Philippians 4:13..._**

We are Christians by Our Love

The people will know that you are a Christian by your love. You are known by the fruit you display. You cannot say that you are an apple tree, but you really produce oranges. ***Matthew 7:16...*** A Christian's life is meant to be a fruitful life. A Christian is full of love, so do not ever imitate this world. ***Romans 12:2...*** The world teaches how to hate. It also teaches how to perpetuate pain and prejudice.

Everything that humanity watches and hears affects them in some way. Acquiring Christ consciousness is a must in a world full of pain and hate. Many people are searching for a true love. Instead of searching for love, be the love. Then, love will find you because you are nothing without displaying compassionate and considerate love. ***1 Corinthians 13:2...***

Relationships are very important in life. Make sure you are fully conscious of yourself before going into a relationship because going into a relationship unconsciously will make it ultimately end in a total disaster. Searching for a partner to meet all of your needs can consume your life. You must be fulfilled inside first; hence, a place where selfishness has no life. If a person enters a relationship with an "I" attitude, is that Christian love? Is that displaying Christian love when a person does that? Or will the love disappear when all of the bottomless-pit needs are not met? If that's the fact, the relationship will be doomed in due time.

Christian love is a place where selfishness and revenge have no life. You must leave this world in the mind to achieve Christian love. Transcend this world in the mind to truly love and find the real you. No one can complete you if you are not complete already through Christ. It's an illusion to wait until the future to be complete and happy. Choose to be happy right now. It's an illusion to wait to love and be the person that you want to be in the future. Be that person right now, because tomorrow is not promised. You cannot make changes in the future. You can only control this very moment. Spread the love of Jesus today.

Be the example of what love really looks like. Show the world what Christian love really is. So again, don't wait for love. Be the love. You are supernatural. Be the spirit inside of you instead of the human being. Human beings can be a sick race at times. Human beings inflict pain on their own so-called loved ones. Every day there are murders, rapes, suicides, and so on. Humans have also killed billions of their own species, not to mention, they trash and plunder the Earth. The beaches, rivers, and oceans are ravaged with trash. Negligent oil companies have killed millions of animals because of reckless oil spills.

Apathetic humans kill innocent animals just for relics or sport and not for food consumption. Why kill a beautiful Lion or Elephant in its luminous environment just for fun? Why kill those animals just for their tusk, tails, or head? Don't they know that they are killing animals that are one with them? The animals are part and parcel of God, too. They are just in different forms of life.

The overexploitation of certain animals affects other species in the ecosystem. Over 41,000 different plants and animals are endangered. Over 16,000 of them are threatened with extinction. Who kills and destroys the very things that are keeping them alive? Who places money before the well-being of the planet and animals? We're all interconnected! We're all one and the same.

Many cultures have been wiped out by mass slaughter, genocidal warfare, and bigotry. *__James 5:6...__* Almost 1.5 million innocent wild buffalos were killed by the U.S. Army alone, almost bringing them into near extinction. The human mind bull doze and cut at least 7 million trees every year, resulting in leaving wildlife without a habitat in which to live. Do these things sound like Christian love? Those are examples of no love!

Would Christian love kill an animal just to put its head on the wall? Of course not! The world must learn how to work side by side with nature and the animals. Is it Christian love to get with someone only because they meet your temporary needs or desires? Then when the thrill is gone, you're gone in the wind? These are only a few examples of perpetual pain and no love.

Do not be the person searching for an illusion. Don't be the person searching and awaiting for a love that only God can supply. Searching for love in all of the wrong places can result into a person having many partners. They're searching for a new high to try. Searching for just the right feeling or pleasure can be extremely draining. No one can make you feel whole except for God. *__Matthew 9:22...__* The physical only supplies short-term peace and happiness.

God loves you more than you love yourself. *__Psalm 86:15...__* It took a lot of planning and compassion for all that you see in existence. God is present everywhere you look. *__Proverbs 15:3...__* Everywhere you look displays His unfailing love for humanity. It's humanity that is making things more difficult in life. It is the human mind creating all of the problems, not God.

Christians have the power to truly love. Christians retains the power to have complete altruism. Display your love every day. Even though the devil will try to steal that away from you. *__John 10:10...__* The devil will give you a situation or problem that stresses you throughout your day. First of all, you have to expose the enemy. Let him know you recognize what he is trying to do. You are not out of your mind. It is the enemy trying to steal your mind and focus off of Jesus. Trying to distract you from the Christian love.

Call the devil out. "Devil, you are a liar and the truth is nowhere in you!" You have to train your mind to focus on Jesus when the enemy comes in. *__1 Thessalonians 5:17...__* Furthermore, to train the mind means to do it more than once. Training is a lifetime process. The more you train, the stronger you will become in Christ, so no positive application is useless. All of it works for you. *__Romans: 8:28...__* Train your mind to love and pray for one another, not hate. *__John 13:34...__* *__James 5:16...__*

How can prejudiced extremist groups like the neo-Nazis and the KKK say they are Christians? They are only masquerading as Christians. Those extremist hate groups believe in the total opposite of Christian love. Those hate groups operate totally on their own fear. Remember, a person can say they are an apple tree, but really produce oranges. Those notorious hate groups are led by Satan and his demons. Satan is going to use these evil, extremist hate groups to stand up against Jesus when He returns. They are just demons in disguise.

Satan's army will not understand the over powering light that Jesus and the Angels emanate. *Revelation 17:12-14... Revelation 18:1-11...* Jesus will cripple Satan's power so that the enemy won't be able to destroy the Earth. *2 Thessalonians 2:8-13... Revelation 20:1...* The enemy is sadistic, psychopathic, and very devious. Humanity needs to expose the enemy and not be misled or provoked by those hate groups. Satan is the biggest deceiver and accuser ever created!

How can you kill someone in Jesus's name? That is sickening and absolutely absurd! "Anyone who hates a brother or sister is a murderer, and you know that no murderer has eternal life residing in him" (*1 John 3:15*). No Christian would kill, lynch, castrate, mutilate, assault, terrorize, gas, hang, beat, assassinate, rape, lie, oppress, burn crosses, burn people, or kill innocent animals just for fun. These evil acts are the (*modus operandi*) of Satan. Christ saves lives. He does not take them.

Christians truly love each other no matter the race or ethnicity. The devil will fill your mind with lies and evil thoughts to contaminate your love. *Philippians 4:8...* Witness only the thoughts and do not react to them. Every time it seems like your mind is getting crowded with foul things, start filling your heart with praise. Start singing every church song that you know to yourself. Start quoting scriptures that you have been practicing to remember. These are examples of your laboring to rest in Christ. The devil will have to release you. Satan and his demons cannot stand peace and Christian love. Demons are afraid of Christ and His mighty power, so they are definitely afraid of you because Christ lives within you. *Matthew 8:29... Ephesians 3:17...*

There is a very powerful story in the Bible when Jesus cast the demons out of a demon-possessed man. **_Mark 5:1-20..._** No one but Jesus was able to heal or cast the demons out of the man. When Jesus encountered the demon-possessed man, the demons started to speak through the man. The demons begged Jesus not to make them leave the area or country.

The demons begged Jesus to cast them into the herd of swine that were grazing nearby. Jesus granted the demons their request to be cast into the swine. When Jesus cast the demons into the swine, the swine immediately ran violently down a steep mountain and drowned. About 2,000 of them perished. Even swine that eat feces cannot stand to be in the presence of gruesome demons. The swine would rather drown themselves. **_Mark 5:13..._** **_Matthew 8:30-32..._**

Never let demons or evil forces distract you from your Christian love. Never let them control your thoughts, because they are perpetual losers and destined for Hell! Let the Spirit of the Lord guide you to love, and replace the human mind with the mind of Christ. Win through your display of "Christian Love". Show the world that you are a Christian by your love. It starts from within.

Victory Is Near, Dry Your Eyes

Don't be afraid of what you are going through. Dry your eyes, victory is near. You are almost there. Situations always gets harder when you are close to your success, so stay strong. Hold your head up and smile. ***Romans 5:3...*** How can you ever achieve victory without a test? Believe in yourself, stay persistent, and you will ultimately win. Under no circumstances feel defeated and lie down. Victory will not come easily. There will be some weary nights, but joy comes in the morning. ***Psalm 30:5...*** Draw your strength from the Lord. You have come too far to turn around now.

You cannot let all of your previous hard work go in vain. If you are thinking about quitting, that would be a major mistake. You will only be hurting yourself more. You would be making the process take longer to reach your goals. Then stress and frustration will set in. If you quit, how will you ever reach the finish line? Keep the finish line in your view. Keep on running toward it even if you stumble. The devil will set out hurdles to slow you down, but those distractions will not work because you are focused on the finish line. Have faith and you will crack the skull of the enemy! ***Judges 9:50-53...*** Keep grinding it out. Your victory is near.

Jesus Is the Plug

Jesus is the plug. Just like as if you were charging your phone. Without that charge, your phone would not work. It is the same way with you and Jesus. Without Jesus inside of you, nothing you do will last. ***John 6:53...*** Let Jesus be your power. Let Jesus be your strength. You have nothing to fear. ***Matthew 28:18...*** Harmonize with Jesus. How can two walk together unless they agree? ***Amos 3:3...***

Download the mind of Jesus Christ. ***Ephesians 4:24...*** Greater is he that is in the Word and not the world. ***1 John 4:4...*** You have to separate yourself from this world. ***John 17:14-16...*** Your old consciousness must be left behind in order to acquire a new one. Your old mind has to be left behind in order to replace it with Christ consciousness.

This world only brings about pain and stress. The flesh loves this world and will put up a big ruckus or fight to stay in it, but you are ultimately the one in control. When you let the world and not the Word take over, you leave yourself open for the devil and his demons to work you anyway they want. You will be like the chaff in the wind, just blowing whatever direction the world goes, doing whatever the world is doing at the time, saying whatever the world is saying. ***Psalm 1:4...*** Following the world and not Christ can drive people into alcoholism, drugs, and other addictive measures. ***Matthew 6:24-34...***

At times, people in this world can frustrate you, but no one else's actions or untamed pain should be able to activate yours. Stay in your Christ consciousness character-mode. True greatness is showing others how to become Christ conscious. You have to stay steady and steadfast when Jesus is your plug. Stay centered! Hold on to your beliefs through the Word. Keep the Word very close to your heart as if it were a treasure. Jesus says to love one another. *__Mark 12:31...__* Your neighbor may be going through a violent storm. Help them out. Your neighbor may have a different religion than you. Pray with and for them. Followers that are plugged into Christ love their neighbors regardless of the situation. So, love. *__John 13:34-35...__*

If someone tries to draw you out of your character, just know Jesus is not being their plug at the time. They are operating in spiritual unconsciousness, but you are not because Jesus is your plug. Thus, you will have a relaxed, calm demeanor, knowing with full assurance that you can do all things and move anything that is in your way. The Holy Word on your tongue will devour the enemy. You will be able to annihilate whoever or whatever comes trying to steal your joy away. Get in your zone of rest where you have been training yourself to go. Your zone of rest should be that you are more than a conqueror and that no weapon formed against you shall prosper. *__Romans 8:37...__* *__Isaiah 54:17...__* Do not worry about how? Just know who the miracle worker is. It is inside you. *__John 14:20...__*

Nothing is off limits to your ability. It is essential not to let people who have not yet figured out who they really are distract you. They need you to be the living demonstration of greatness. It is truly a gift to be plugged into Christ. *__John 15:1-9...__* Jesus said, "I am the vine; you are the branches. If you remain in me and I in you, you will bear much fruit; apart from me you can do nothing" (*__John 15:5 NIV__*).

Many people live their whole lives stressed out, angry, and defeated, resulting in creating sicknesses within themselves. Saying defeatist things and complaining is a sure way to kill blessings. When you let Jesus be your plug, you can do anything. Therefore, stay plugged into Him perpetually.

Your Faith Will Be Sufficient

Hold on to your faith, my sisters and brothers. Hold on! Your faith is sufficient. All you need is the faith of a mustard seed. ***Matthew 17:20...*** Stop waiting for everything to be perfect or just right. You just have to trust in the process. When things get rough in life, you are just being tested. Your faith will be tested in the storm. Mount up like an awe-inspiring eagle and fly above the storm. The eagle uses the winds of the storm to soar majestically.

Stay solid in the mind. Never hesitate or be afraid to dream big because your blessings are within the vision that you have. Where there is no vision, the people will perish. ***Proverbs 29:18...*** Call things out that you want in life. Speak life into them. Speak like you already have them. ***Romans 4:17...*** Act like you know you cannot fail. Everybody is not going to visualize what you see. Everyone will not be able to understand your greatness at work. However, you cannot let that hinder you.

Unfortunately, not everyone is interested in fulfilling their dreams or in seeing you fulfill yours, either. Some people are satisfied with mere mediocrity. Being average just will not do for people who seek and scratch for greatness. Faith is the engine that propels you to success. Without it, nothing you do will please God. ***Hebrews 11:6...*** So do not say, "When I get more faith, I will do this or that." Start now with the faith that you have! It is okay to live free and have authority in Christ. ***Matthew 28:18-20...*** Your faith is sufficient.

You are healed right now before a sickness even comes about. It is absolutely necessary not to wait until a sickness comes. Claim victory now! ***1 Corinthians 15:57...*** Your display of thanksgiving is your faith.

Activate your faith all day, every day. It is sufficient. Make faith who you are as a person. Remember, Jesus gave humanity the power to do it. It is up to you to believe that you already have the power through Him. (The Power Source) It is completely up to you to tap into His power and utilize it. (The Plug) You are who you believe you are. You are the child of the Holy King. ***2 Corinthians 4:6...*** You are royalty! Act, walk, and talk like it. Your faith is already sufficient.

Im Successful

Wake up every day saying that you are successful. Say, "I have riches and prosperity in this house." Say, "I am truly blessed." Always claim victory every day! Doing this will release your faith into the spiritual realm. Never use your words carelessly because it only hurts you and others around you. It is best not to speak unless you are speaking the Word or something uplifting. ***Matthew 12:36...*** Your life is the total sum of what you say and believe.

Even if you are not seeing success right now. Plan ahead for greatness and success. ***Luke 14:28... Proverbs 21:5...*** You must have the courage to attain the unattainable. Remember, when you plan ahead, always ask the Lord for His will to be done. ***James 4:15-16...*** Program your conscience and mouth for success. Never wait until you are successful to act like it. Start right now! That is showing the Lord that your faith is in what He is about to do in your life. You may ask, "How am I successful? I work for minimum wages." Do not let money and wealth determine how you feel about yourself because, after all money and wealth are material things. ***Matthew 6:25...*** For the value of wisdom is far more valuable than silver or gold. ***Proverbs 8:11...***

Be your purpose in life and not your occupation. What if Jesus would have come to the Earth just to be a carpenter? He would have only been a great carpenter, and no one on Earth would be saved. But, Jesus knew what His purpose was. He lived in His purpose! ***Luke 19:10...*** His purpose was to save all of humanity from the enemy's hands. ***John 12:44-50...*** Jesus obliterated all of the evil destruction Satan had planned for humanity. Jesus makes His followers successful because He is the most successful one of them all.

You must realize that you are a supernatural being, having a human experience. Enjoy the experience of being in a human body. Learn all of the lessons that has been put in front of you. Your soul will live on while material things will fade away to ashes. To be successful in this life, you must be thoroughly focused on enriching your soul and not things that will perish. Not believing that you are successful can be draining to your soul. That is why it is pivotal to lean on Christ and practice every day to be successful like Him.

Christ says, "Do not be troubled by the things of this world." ***John 14:1...*** He said, "Lay all of your cares upon Him." ***1 Peter 5:7...*** Furthermore, that means if you lay all of your problems upon Him, you should always be in peace. Leave all of your burdens upon the Lord and He will give you rest. ***Matthew 11:28...*** Jesus goes before you every day planning out your day for you to be successful. So it does not matter what happens that day. Jesus has you in His comforting arms. Believe and never doubt.

The opposition wants you to be distracted from your successes and dreams. That is the last thing that the enemy wants. Just think: If everyone lived in their purpose and used their gifts and talents, this world would be a heaven on Earth. Everyone would be successful and great. But in this world, everyone is competing against each other. They are competing against each others' beliefs and religions. People are also trying to outshine the other with worthless material items. All gifts, talents, and successes comes from the Lord. ***James 1:17...***

Never be comfortable doing average things. There is something extra special about you. There is something special that makes you stand out from other people. You just have to identify what that gift is. You have to figure out what gift separates you from everyone else. Your success is in your difference. God made you different for a reason. Embrace it! What is your gift and purpose in life? Start using it for your good and for humanity. The world needs you. The Lord needs you, despite what any detractors may say or think. Believe in you!

That big company that you are working for already found their success and greatness. What is your greatness? Life is too short to start working towards greatness and success tomorrow. Start right now. Start mapping out your plan right now. Get up and move! You owe that to you and your family. Leave a legacy upon the Earth through Christ. Only what you do for Him will have any sustainability or meaning.

You have to include Christ in whatever makes you different. He has to be involved with your successes. Therefore, attach Him to what you are doing at all times. That is called "Real True Success". Success is in the mind and in action. As soon as you decide that you are successful, you will act like it. You will also start to walk and talk like it. You are already destined for success. So the only person keeping you away from it is you and your thinking.

Get to a quiet space and take some time to meditate. Quiet meditation time and getting away from all distractions is very essential. Run or flee away from all distractions. Start speaking and visualizing success. Say, "I am great." "I am successful through Jesus Christ. I embrace my difference. I am successful." Focus on what makes you different. Then, start working on it diligently. You are successful.

Seven Is the Number of Divine Completion
God's Divine Number

Chapter Seven

<u>Perfect Peace</u>

On Your Way to Greatness

Religion

Religion: The belief in and worship of a superhuman controlling power, especially a personal god or gods. Religion: Religion is to know God and to love God. What part of this definition means to battle and fight each other? What part of this definition requires a Holy War? The Lord does not need anyone to pull a gun for Him. God does not have a religion. What part of religion said to have thousands of different denominations?

Religion shouldn't separate humanity. In all actuality, it should unite humanity. The intent of religion is to bring every corner of the world together to serve God. Religions should be working together in harmony like a well-oiled machine. Religion is humanity's gift and invites all cultures to come together and love God. Infidels? No one is insignificant. Everyone has a place in this world.

Humanity should not have lack of love for one another because of differences in religion. That is like making religion out to be some sort of gang. Everybody is in his or her so-called groups against one another, trying to prove which one is better. Why can't we all agree to disagree? Do not miss out on your fellow sisters' and brothers' love. We can all learn a great deal from each other. True knowledge is learning about all cultures and walks of life. Isolating yourself to only one set of ideals and ignoring everyone else's could be a detriment. You learn more about your God through other cultures. And once other cultures are learned, you may soon discover or realize that we are all serving the same God. It is just done in different ways.

Most religions have a very fascinating story about God. God can change into many forms, but there is only one God. *1 Corinthians 8:4...* God is infinite and it is not feasible to know everything about Him, but every true servant of the Lord must vow to know everything about Him. It may take an eternity, but your spirit has time. Always think the impossible. *Isaiah 40:28...*

The Srimad-Bhagavatam, in the Hindu religion, has a very compelling story written about the universe. The Srimad-Bhagavatam explains how half of the universe is water, and the other half is mostly empty. Maha-Vishnu is the creator and protector of the universe, based on the Hindu religion. When Maha-Vishnu exhale, all of the material elements and universes are formed. For example, when Maha-Vishnu exhales, planets and stars are formed. Then, when Maha-Vishnu inhales, all of the universes are destroyed and merged back into His body.

One breath of Maha-Vishnu lasts for 310 trillion solar years. According to the Srimad-Bhagavatam, the universe is halfway there and has existed for 155 trillion years. The Srimad-Bhagavatam explains the science of God in detail and His many creations. Recently, scientists have found that the universe is filled with some type of super fluid. A super fluid? A fluid that has very unusual qualities was discovered. This super fluid allows waves and photons to travel like sound in the air. Life would not exist if there were no photons or waves.

Scientists have come to the conclusion that whatever is powering this phenomenon is of zero viscosity, which means that this super fluid phenomenon cannot be stopped or slowed down in any way. This super fluid flows indefinitely throughout the universe. These giant discoveries prove that the ancients of old had some highly technical advanced knowledge of the universe.

The ancient text of the Srimad-Bhagavatam explains in detail what science has just recently discovered. The text also explains the reason for reincarnation. The Hindu religion explains that the purpose for human life is for self-realization and achieving Krishna consciousness. And if a person desires worthless material items and acts like an animal, they can. But in the next life, they will experience life as an animal.

Also, in the Hindu religion there is a dormant power that lies within everyone known as "Kundalini". The Kundalini energy is said to be located at the base of the spine. Once Kundalini is awakened, it will lead into a higher consciousness and spiritual enlightenment. There is a very interesting Hindu and Buddhist term called "Samadhi". Samadhi means "a state of being totally aware of the present moment." Samadhi requires higher levels of concentration and meditation. You must let go of the world and allow the old self to die to achieve Samadhi. The outside world does not affect someone with Samadhi because complete equanimity will be achieved. Equanimity means "mental calmness, composure, and evenness of temper, especially in a difficult situation."

The Pistis Sofia is a very intriguing text that was written between the third and fourth centuries AD. According to Wikipedia, "In this text, the risen Jesus spent 11 years speaking with His disciples, teaching them only the lower mysteries. After the 11 years, Jesus receives His true garment and is able to reveal the higher mysteries revered by the disciples. The prized mysteries relates to complex cosmologies and knowledge necessary for the soul to reach the higher divine realms."

In the third book of the Pistis Sofia, chapter 102, Jesus was speaking with His disciples and said, "When I shall have gone into the Light, then herald it to the whole world and say unto them: Cease not to seek day and night and remit not yourselves unto ye find the mysteries of the Light-kingdom which will purify you and make you into refined light and lead you into the Light-kingdom. Renounce the whole world and the whole matter therein and all its care and all its sins, in a word all of the associations which are in it, that ye may be worthy of the mysteries of the Light and be saved of all the chastisements which are in the judgements."

In this important text of the Pistis Sofia, Jesus explains to His disciples that your whole life should be dedicated to the Word of God and obeying the Ten Commandments so that you will have a place in the Light-kingdom. Therefore, God and His Son has to mean more than life to an individual. The Pistis Sofia has troves of life-changing information.

"The Shroud of Turin" is a mysterious linen cloth bearing the image of the face of Jesus. The measurements of this baffling shroud is 14.5 feet by 3.5 feet. This incredible cloth is believed to be the shroud that was wrapped around Jesus in the tomb after the crucifixion. The shroud has been subjected to heavy analysis and have also been radiocarbon dated. The Shroud of Turin is the most tested religious relic in the world. The mishandling of the shroud in the past has increased the curiosity of its authenticity.

The Shroud of Turin is kept in the royal chapel of the Cathedral of Saint John the Baptist in Turin, northern Italy. Many expert analysts have come to the conclusion that the shroud cannot possibly be a hoax. Many scientists have come to the realization that the image could have only materialized from a radiant light flash, a radiant light flash that produced a finely detailed negative photographic image. Four gospels in the Bible mentions Jesus being buried in a "fine linen cloth". *Matthew 27:59-60... Mark 15:46... Luke 24:12... John 20:1-8...*

In the Quran it states, "Your ally is none but Allah and [therefore] His Messenger and those who have believed – those who established prayer and give zakah (tithe), and they bow in [worship]. And whoever is an ally of Allah and His Messenger and those who believed - indeed the party of Allah - they will be predominant." *Quran 5:55-56...* Whoever loves and believes in God and His Messenger is a party of God. Therefore, a Holy War is not necessary. The Resurrection, End of the Age, Rapture, The Harvest, or The Day of Enlightenment will handle non-believers. The Angels are going to separate the good individuals from the bad ones on the Earth. *Matthew 13:49-52... Matthew 13:38-39...*

Knowledge of other religions can be an asset to your life. The purpose of life is to transform into a body of light, a body full of love. *Matthew 13:43...* This life must be for the preparation of ascension. (The Rapture) (The End of the Age) It means everything to find you a home in glory. (Heaven) *Matthew 24:37-42... Luke 17:24-37...* The teachings of the Lord should not be downplayed as only a myth or imagination. Those who fail to live in constant expectation of the rapture will be severely disappointed when the "*last day*" actually arrives and they are not spiritually prepared. ***Matthew 13:36-43... Daniel 12:1-4...***

"Listen, I will tell you a mystery: We will not all sleep, but we will all be changed-in a flash, in a twinkling of an eye, at the last trumpet. For the trumpet will sound, the dead will be raised imperishable, and we will be changed" (*1 Corinthians 15:51 NIV*). ***1 Corinthians 15:51-57...*** Humanity will be shown clearly all the thoughts and actions of their lifetimes at the time of the resurrection. ***Revelation 20:12... Revelation 21:27...***

It is only a myth to believe if religion were taken out of the world that it would be a better place. Prayer has been proven through quantum physics to make positive, supernatural changes within the consciousness of humanity. When mass congregations pray or meditate together, crime and murders have been found to decrease drastically in those areas.

Prayer reaches far into the depths of time/space. According to star-stuffs.com, "Quantum physics even suggests that by re-directing our focus and our attention we can bring about a new course of events." This process is known as "quantum interconnectedness". Many prominent scientists have proven, experienced, and spoken about the miraculous power of prayer. The United States have been severely feeling the consequences of banning prayer out of the public schools. Statistics show that there has been a major escalation in gang activity, sexual transmitted diseases, rape, childhood pregnancy, illiteracy, suicide, mass shootings, and so on. A world without religion or prayer would make this planet a very terrifying and lawless place to be.

Expand your thinking. Expand your Love. True religion is to understand and love God. That does not make you weak. In fact, that makes you very strong because humanity is much stronger together as a team. We all need to work together as one unit under God. Instead, now we have set up a system in life called the American Dream, in which we are all competing against each other. Many billionaires and millionaires are just hoarding their riches, stepping all over the needy, hungry, and homeless. **_Matthew 6:2... Jeremiah 20:13... James 5:1-9..._** There is nothing wrong with the generation of wealth as long as it is achieved honestly and used for good and charitable purposes.

Many religions practice and focus on what the individual can do to please God. Those religions are performance based. Christianity is the opposite. Christianity focuses on the blood of Christ. In Him, His sheep are made holy. **_Hebrews 10:1-18..._** Christianity focuses on the finished works of Christ to please God. Let God guide you to do what is right. Everyone will have a different journey with God. No two experiences will be the same. It is like a fingerprint.

Is it right to kill someone because they do not believe in what you believe? Is it right to oppress women and make them feel worthless? Is it right to kill someone because they are gay? Society needs to love one another no matter what. No one can check if you gave your soul to God. The people will know by the fruit you display that you gave your soul to God.

The enemy must be defeated. Your religion should teach you how to defeat the enemy. It is the ego plus the enemy that makes you feel hate for one another. **_Titus 3:3..._** Resist the enemy and make him flee. **_James 4:7..._** Allow your religion or the knowledge of other religions to be an asset to you. Let's celebrate and embrace the diversity of humanity. Your god should not get mad if you prayed for a neighbor that is not your same religion. Your god should not get mad if you loved someone in spite of who or what they believe. Treat everyone with dignity and compassion. We are all family no matter what religion people have.

We are all living in a human body. We are just different shades of the same color because of melanin in our bodies. Right and wrong is a choice. Good always trumps evil. Let us be a team regardless of differences in religion or race. Let us team up, "Team Love". Let us not be afraid of each other. Let us learn a great amount of knowledge and respect all cultures. An individual can develop a different outlook on life by learning from other cultures. We are all family, let us be happy with each other. Love conquers all. Let "Religion" unite humanity, not divide us.

Trouble

The fear of man is a snare, but the one who trusts in the Lord will be kept safe. **_Proverbs 29:25..._** Everything in life is ultimately controlled by God. He sits on high. Things that we call trouble are just life circumstances. The trouble or storm was set up on purpose. Negativity can be used to make positivity in some instances. For example, God closes doors, only to open up a new one for you. He closes doors to make us progress and to take a different path. We are His children.

When things start to unfold that you do not understand and seems abnormal, do not worry. God is just up to something. He is just up to His blessing ways as usual. ("A divine set up!") Trust Him! Even your storms are by design. This process in the Lord can be confusing at times because you do not know exactly what He is doing at the moment. And it may be quite uncomfortable. Every issue that comes about has a rational lesson involved. Do not miss it by complaining. Instead, look for the lesson. Remember, there is a blessing in the storm.

Perfect Peace does not necessarily mean that trouble will not come. It just means when trouble does come your way, you will be able to stand in "Perfect Peace". **_Hebrews 13:5-8..._** You are molded through the experiences and troubles in your life, but never let them break you. Learn valuable lessons from your life experiences and do not be afraid of them. You cannot fear anything in this life. Why? Because God did not give us a spirit of fear; but of power, and of love, and of a sound mind. **_2 Timothy 1:7..._** That means you already know that you are going to be kept safe. Those things that are called problems are just life situations.

Whenever you stop worrying about the end or how things are going to unfold, that is when things start to happen in your life. It is essential to let God be your strength through times of trouble. Trouble makes you grateful for the good times. Jesus will be there right on time. Every time. There will never be another love like His. **_Romans 8:38..._** His peace surpasses all understanding. **_Philippians 4:7..._** These are not just great quotes or a figure of speech. Jesus is *"real!"* His peace and love is impenetrable! His love will have you wondering why you are so happy and free.

When trouble comes about, be encouraged. Use it as a chance to conquer and divide. Through Jesus you can be as bold as a lion. **_Daniel 6:23..._** No flinch or fear will ever be in you. You will be able to withstand any situation. You cannot look at other's situations and think you will have the same outcome. You are anointed and appointed. Yes, someone else may have died from some type of disease. That does not mean that you are going to accept the same fate. Your faith will heal you no matter what the enemy says. Have some "now faith". Now Faith: Absolute faith right now, in God's ability and His love for you. Your faith in that you are already healed is all you need. **_Matthew 9:20-22... Matthew 10:1-8... Ephesians 1:3..._**

Trouble can only exist if you fear and feed it. Face trouble nose to nose. Let trouble know that your peace cannot be touched. Stay grounded in your mind. With Jesus, you will be at peace. Labor to rest in Him. **_Hebrews 4:11..._** It may take a little work to realize who you are in Christ, or it may not, because through repeated unconscious acts, the ego is fed. The more the ego is fed, the stronger it becomes. Feeding the ego makes you self-dependent, instead of God-dependent. Everything on the outside will matter more to a person with a giant ego. For instance, physical appearance, money, clothes, cars, homes, drugs, relationships, and sex, etc. Too much focus on these things will lead to trouble.

It is just pivotal that you get to that place of rest, a place where you are fully conscious, fully aware of your emotions and feelings. Through trouble you have to trust your Father to do exactly what He said. After all, He is God. He said, "Cast all of your cares upon Him." ***Matthew 11:28...*** So are you wrong for literally doing that when trouble comes about? Are you lazy for letting Jesus pull strings in your life while you rest? Absolutely not. You are following what Jesus said do. Get out of His way and rest. You get in Jesus's way when you start worrying about the outcome of a thing. It is okay to work hard for success, but just do not worry about the outcome. When you rest, He works.

Relax. Stop trying to operate and orchestrate everything on your own. Instead, take everything unto Christ. ***Philippians 4:6...*** He has all of the answers. He knows your future and direction. You do not. Do not walk right into trouble or bump your head going in your own direction. The Word is your rest and compass. When you develop this type of faith, trouble will not even be trouble anymore. This world and its troubles will no longer effect or move you in any direction. Most of the things that would have bothered you before rest will not trouble you at all now. You will laugh at trouble. Actually, you will laugh at the old you in the past. You will be full of exuberance because no trouble will be able to shake your faith anymore.

Be bold and unfearful of anything, just as when Shadrach, Meshach, and Abednego had faith in God when they were in trouble. ***Daniel 3:1-30...*** They had supreme faith in God, even when they were faced with an excruciating death in the fiery furnace. With faith Shadrach, Meshach, and Abednego came out of the fiery furnace with no harm done to their bodies. Their robes were not scorched and there was not a smell of fire anywhere on them. Not a single hair on their heads were singed in the fire. Stand strong in the Lord. Be anchored in Him so that nothing can pull you away from your faith. Trouble? I say peace beyond your understanding. ***Mark 4:38-40...***

Pride

Pride: A feeling of deep pleasure or satisfaction derived from one's own achievements. One's own achievements? Let pride and ego go, and replace them with humility. ***Proverbs 11:2...*** Humble yourselves before the Lord. Pride gets in the way of your becoming humble. Pride can destroy your greatness completely because pride helps you develop a self-attitude, which is contrary to the Word of God.

Pride will have you mad at people for no reason at all. That is because pride and ego looks for and feeds on confrontations. It has an "I wish a person would" type of attitude. Pride and ego wear a big chip on their shoulders, daring anyone to knock it off! Pride and ego must be checked at the door. Drop it! It holds you down and is a dream-destroyer. It also makes you focus on things that are totally worthless.

All of your achievements were not because of you. God gave you all that you have. ***Romans 12:4... 1 Peter 4:10...*** Never feel that you have done things all on your own. Instead, know that God supplied you through it all. ***James 1:17...*** You can never achieve "Perfect Peace" with pride because it will always steal your joy away in the end. Satan is the prideful one that loves to snatch up your joy and peace. Never hold on to things which are wrong. If you do not have anything good to say, just stay quiet until you do. There is nothing wrong with that. Help a neighbor in need when you can. Make yourself available for someone other than yourself. ***Matthew 25:44-45...*** Spread the love of Jesus around wherever you go. ***Matthew 5:16...*** Spreading the love of Jesus is a great way to annihilate pride and ego.

Your brain is wired to be connected to the Lord, and not to the world.

Pride or ego will short-circuit your connection to Him. Remember the prideful, worldly mind is not the real you. You may say, "Yes, this is the real me." No, it is not the real you. Christ consciousness is the real you, where love, compassion, and spiritual integrity conquers all evil. Pride and ego have their own personality traits that are opposite to Christ consciousness. Humanity has forgotten their origin, just like a giant case of amnesia. The devil has set up all of his traps and systems to program the minds of people. The systems of the devil promotes pride and contaminates the spiritual morals and ethics of mankind. *1 John 3:8...*

Now is the time to overthrow the prideful devil and his nuclear weapons. It is time for a "Spiritual Revolution". The time is now to dislodge anyone that is not in favor of love, equality, justice, and peace. *Jeremiah 22:13...* The indifference to pride and hatred will not be tolerated in this "New World Revolution". The New World Revolution will incorporate and hold on to the loving traditions that reach back and lift up those that have fallen. The New World Revolution will hold on to the legacies and traditions that love the senior citizen, orphan, handicapped, veteran, widow, hopeless, poor, sick, rebuked, spat upon, and the devalued in this society.

Jesus is coming sooner than anyone thinks because His children are about to create heaven on Earth. Guns and nukes will not be able to penetrate this New Revolution. This New World Revolution and awakening will be in full pursuit of justice, honor, decency, and spiritual unity. It is time to recognize and appreciate the real heroes of this world. Let us cherish and memorialize the memories of the ones that have suffered from the hands of the oppressor. *Jeremiah 22:3...* Remembrance should be for the ones who summoned enough strength from within to rise up for freedom and justice. Those are the real heroes. *Revelation 17:6...* Those are the heroes that should be taught about in today's school systems.

The school system should teach the stories about the hideous acts performed against humanity. The New World Revolution school system will focus on the full development of the individual student. Every student will be thoroughly evaluated by a licensed professional because most of the students that are considered mentally ill, retarded, or learning disabled in the public school systems are not mentally ill at all. No student will be left behind. Gifts and talents will be able to flourish in an environment that encourages creativity and free thinking instead of senseless, outdated classes chosen by the politicians. There will be no more robot human beings when this revolution takes place. Everyone will be free to love and make a full contribution to the world.

Who places the prideful individuals that are prejudiced, genocidal murderers, sexual predators, oppressors, war-crime dictators, and sadistic slave owners on a pedestal? Does it make any sense to erect statues and celebrate holidays for these felonious, unconscious beings? Does how many people you hurt and kill make you great now in this world? Why should individuals of pride, hate, and bigotry be placed on the front of money? Why are xenophobic criminals elected and placed in charge of justice? Humanity must rise up and take a stand against Satan so that the world can live in peace, and topple the evil systems of the enemy.

Throughout history, millions of indigenous people and slaves have been wiped out by pride and hate. Their resources were ravaged and their lands were stolen. Many of the oppressed fallen were mutilated, slaughtered, and raped by the individuals that have statues erected all over the world. Horrific concentration camps and gas chambers were used to torture millions of Jews in the Holocaust. Those murderers and oppressors are Satan's favorite people. Pride and hate is the M.O. of the devil. The devil wants these hate criminals to be your favorite people and so-called forefathers.

Statues of hate criminals should be placed in a museum because they are still relevant to history. Statues of the people who fought for love and peace on the planet should remain in full view. It is time for humanity to wake up! ***Ephesians 5:14...*** The Lord made you to be a free thinker, not a robot. As long as humanity goes along with the status quo of pride and evil, the longer humanity will remain in bondage. Satan cannot make humanity conform to his evil ways. Humanity is conforming willingly and unknowingly. *Revelation 12:9...*

The time is now to make a huge paradigm shift and kick pride out of your life because pride takes you out of the will of God. Also, remember that the opposition is watching you closely. The enemy wants you to hold on to your old prideful ways. Pride and ego will be saying things to you such as, "Do not leave me." "Oh, you will be back again." "You need money, not love." "Why worry about anyone else?" "Get yours!" "This is just how the world is." "You cannot change the world." "Who do you think you are?" "You need me to protect you from this mean and terrible world." "You have to look mad so that people will not mess with you." "Curse people out because it makes you feel good and gets rid of your stress." Those are only a few lies of the insidious enemy. *John 8:44...*

The devil will send his people in droves, trying to snatch up the Perfect Peace for which you have labored. Therefore, stay in the Spirit. *Matthew 13:19...* Do what you know is right and never let pride or ego set in. "Pride goes right before destruction, and has a haughty spirit before a fall" (*Proverbs 16:18 NIV*). This means that pride is a major set-up for the fall of a person. It is in the Word of God.

If you feel that you have been disrespected or cheated on in a relationship, do not let pride set in and get you upset. Listen to your heart and have compassion because pride and ego will block your vision and all rationality. Let the person explain themselves while you let the Spirit guide you. Then you will begin to see the real issue very clearly. The devil will use someone that you love or admire to distract you, especially if you are experiencing a "Christ Euphoria"!

(*Warning!*) A Christ euphoria is when you get a sudden burst of adrenaline that lasts all day. You may just start laughing or singing out of nowhere because the Christ euphoria feels so good! You will start to feel like you can accomplish anything in this world. You may even start to cry tears of joy for no reason when you are experiencing a Christ euphoria. It is a feeling that words cannot describe and surpasses all understanding! A Christ euphoria raises up the red flag for the devil and his demons to come test you. Meditate on your favorite scripture while being tested because that is all it will ever be. A test.

Never let people with pride destroy what you have scratched and worked hard for. You have worked hard to achieve the mind of Christ. *1 Corinthians 2:16...* (Your original mind...) Its hard work because your worldly mind will always be there waiting on you to relent, waiting on you to let up on your praying and meditating with God. *Psalm 1:2...* Stand for what is right and denounce what is wrong because pride and ego is on its way down to a devastating fall. *Luke 18:9-14...*

Thank You, Lord!

There is something very special about always giving the Lord thanks because after all, He has been *"so"* good! **_Psalm 34:8..._** Suppress worrying about what you are seeing or feeling right now. **_Habakkuk 3:17-18..._** You cannot ever let your feelings get in the way of giving thanks. Even when things go all wrong, start giving thanks to God immediately. That will confuse the enemy. The enemy wants you to dwell on anything but the Lamb's power or blood. You have to remember, Jesus is the one that tells the waves of the oceans to behave. **_Mark 4:39... Matthew 8:27..._** When Jesus says "peace," there will be peace. Therefore, you already know in confidence that your Lord will come through.

There is no failure in Christ. Hold on to your faith if the doctor comes with an unfavorable diagnosis because you know who the master physician is. Jesus will be with you in the midst of it all. He is the Way, Truth, and the Life. **_John 14:6..._** By His stripes you are healed. **_Isaiah 53:5..._** There is no way around those promises. Take Jesus at His Word and stand on it.

There is so much to be thankful for. Jesus has protected you from an inestimable amount of harm. Daily! **_2 Samuel 22:3-4..._** If it were really known how much He has protected and covered His sheep, Christians and nonbelievers would probably get lightheaded from the news. Jesus Christ's blood covers everyone that has ever lived, but it is up to the individual to recognize it and follow Him into Perfect Peace. **_Ephesians 1:4-5... John 8:12..._** "Thank you, Lord, for all of your protection. You have continued to make a way out of no way." Speaking that is letting your spirit know that you depend totally on Christ and not yourself.

Thank Him every day that you wake up because if you woke up, you still have a destiny to fulfill. Your blessing is in your praise and thanksgiving unto the Lord. **_Psalm 100:4..._** Thanksgiving displays your faith. When someone promises to give you a gift in the future, you automatically say thank you right then, even though, you have not received the gift yet. Would you trust someone else more than you trust God? Wait on God's gift for you. Thank Him right now in advance for His many blessings. Trust God and His promises. They will come to pass.

If you would just be faithful with the least or a little, God will turn it into much. "The least" or "the little" is equivalent to your money. ("Your Tithe.") It does not matter how much money it is. Jesus will honor it and turn it into much. **_Luke 21:1-4..._** God will supply you with an abundance. **_Matthew 25:23..._** **_Luke 16:1-13..._** Jesus says, "That the tithe requires the *'least'* of your faith or trust in the kingdom," the *"least"* of your faith before healing, prosperity, protection, peace, or anything else that you may desire from the Kingdom.

Giving worthless money requires the *"least"* amount of faith. Therefore, trust God with your tithe, *"**the least**"* because He entrusted you with the money that you have. Your occupation produces your seed. Honor Him with your seed. **_Genesis 4:4..._** God covers and protects your mind, family, friends, health, home, and vehicle, etc... How could you ever trust God for healing if you do not trust Him with the least/money? He loves you no matter what! The tithe simply displays your love and trust in Him. Your tithe says, "Thank you, Lord!"

So whether you have a little or a lot, give out of love for Him even if you have to cut back on some things. The poor widow only gave two mites in the book of Mark. But Jesus said that she gave more than anyone else in the treasury. Everyone else gave out of an abundance of their wealth. She gave out of poverty. She gave all that she had to the Lord. The widow trusted totally in Jesus. She just wanted to say, "Thank You, Lord!" That is why she gave more in the sight of Jesus. It was the amount of trust and love she gave. It was not the amount of currency that mattered to Jesus. ***Mark 12:42-43...*** He will take of you, tithe or no tithe. Believers tithe and give from their hearts simply because they love Him.

"O give thanks, and let the redeemed of the Lord say so!" ***Psalm 107:1-2...*** Even give thanks to the Lord when He disciplines you because whom He loves, He corrects. ***Proverbs 3:11-12...*** Thanksgiving opens up your heart, so give thanks under any condition. If you cannot talk, just write "Thank you, Lord." It is okay to allow yourself to shed tears of joy. Lift up your hands and say, "I love you Lord!" Just start giving thanks right now because He has been that good. Jesus loves that, and He loves you unconditionally.

Lose Your Mind

People will ponder, how can you stand through the storm? But not only able to stand through storms, but you can speak to the storms and make them behave. **_Mark 4:39..._ _Matthew 8:27..._** A Christian can stand beautifully through any mental or physical storm because they already know with full assurance that no hurt, harm, or danger can stand against them.

The very things that would make most people cringe and cry will make you laugh. It does not matter what type of disaster strikes, Christians know that they have a nice cozy place to reside. People all around you will think that you have lost your mind. Just tell them that you have lost your mind because you have the mind of Christ now! **_1 Corinthians 2:16..._** You have been transformed by the renewing of your mind. **_Romans 12:2..._**

There is no way to renew something that you've never had. How can you restore something you've never had in the first place? Renew or restored means to return something to its original condition. The Word of God is specific and precise. Furthermore, that means that you have already had the mind of Christ before the fall of Adam. You just do not remember the fall, just like you do not remember being in your mother's womb, but it definitely happened. Moreover, this is where knowing who and whose you are comes in handy.

You must question everything you have been told in the past and find yourself. You are supernatural! You have always been. Do not hold your spirit hostage thinking carnally like the world. **_1 Corinthians 2:14..._** There are two minds inside of you that are at work, a Christ mind and a worldly mind. Which one do you follow? **_Romans 8:5..._**

Recently, there was a research study done on the effects of poverty on individuals. The research study found that poverty-stricken individuals had an earlier death rate than wealthy individuals. At first, the researchers thought it was because the poverty-stricken people just could not afford health care and other necessities. But this was not the case. Only a third of the poverty deaths was the result of scarce provisions and no money for healthcare. Even poverty-stricken individuals in other rich countries with free healthcare died earlier than the wealthier individuals.

The study came to the conclusion that the poor people died not from lack of provisions and healthcare, but because they felt poor. It was completely in the minds of the poverty-stricken individuals. Poverty was in their minds. They were thinking in their worldly, carnal mind. They were thinking poor instead of prosperity in the name of Jesus. Lose the poverty mind because the mind is very powerful. The worldly mind can cost people their fruitful life.

There is a very peculiar phenomenon, called the placebo effect. The placebo effect is a fake medical treatment to sick patients. The doctor would prescribe something like sugar pills for a disease or some other serious medical condition. Most of the patient's condition would improve or be eliminated through this placebo effect. The pills were fake. They were just sugar pills. But the patients believed that they were healed or vastly improved in their minds. The mind is extremely powerful. If you believe you are healed, you will be healed! *John 5:6-10...*

The opposite of placebo effect is nocebo effect. The nocebo effect is the patient having no faith in being healed. Their condition only worsens. Some of the nocebo-effect patients were just not seeing a change in their health fast enough. So they lost all hope. The nocebo effect is a worldly mind at its best. A person must stay positive and believe they can be healed no matter how long it takes. The Nocebo-effect patients were possibly saying defeatist things like, "I will never get better." "These pills and medication will never help my condition." "Why don't I just die and get it over with." "God does not love me." "Jesus's stripes cannot heal my ailment or disease." These lies are unfathom- ably false!

Lose the mind that has any doubt in the blood. It is unacceptable to let the enemy win. Sometimes you may have to endure the storm until the sun shines. After the storm dissipates, there will be a beautiful rainbow. This means to hold on through the tough times. Your relief is on the way. Wait the storm out, and let Jesus be your sunshine in darkness and shelter in the rain. Everything you say, see, hear, and feel has a direct effect on you. Negative thoughts and stress have a direct impact on the molecular structure within the body.

A worldly mind only creates stress and emotional pain. Negative thoughts, anxiety, and stress prevents certain areas of the brain from growing properly. Doubt and unrest within the body can stunt the growth of the hippocampus in the brain. A worldly mind is only a det- riment and a bloody murderer. Lose it! The worldly mind is not even the real you. The worldly mind's happiness is very short-lived. It only experiences joy and pleasure in short spurts. The worldly mind is al- ways in search and feeds on more. It never appreciates the moment. You must learn how to separate the two minds.

Start watching how you react to different situations. Do not be harsh or critical. Just observe and analyze your actions. Become fully aware of your emotions and everything that is going on around you. Are your actions mirroring Christ, or what the world is doing? The worldly mind is trapped in time. It is always shifting back and forth between the past and future. Consequently, it is always searching for unrest and conflict.

A worldly mind is always irritated when things do not go as planned. Christ-minded people just accept what is and trust in the Lord. The worldly mind fights against situations and is always over-thinking. Christ-minded people just change the situation by using their author- ity. It is as simple as that! The Christ mind does not have to over-think anything. Instead, the Christ mind already has a solution through the Holy Spirit: "The Word."

Never let the worldly/carnal mind play tricks on you because it will not ever let you rest. *__2 Corinthians 10:4-8...__* The worldly mind is greedy and will not ever be satisfied. It is like a bottomless pit that loves to be fed constantly. The traps of the devil were set up long before you were upon the Earth. *__1 John 3:8...__* He is very crafty. He has been a liar and a murderer since the beginning of time. Satan will say that you do not need Christ consciousness for Perfect Peace.

You have to step out of the mind and observe it. Do not be judgmental of your worldly mind. Just observe it. This process will begin to get you out of your body and into peaceful oneness. This is a very important step to follow because you will start to correct your negative actions and thoughts. Negative thoughts and actions will begin to diminish when attention is brought to them.

Everything is done by faith in Jesus, the merciful-minded. Everything should be done through His Holy name. Lose the mind that has doubts and trust the power of the Lord. Get the mind of Christ, where all things are possible. *__Philippians 4:13...__* It is a totally different frequency or dimension living with the Prince of Peace. You will know exactly when you are starting to use your Christ mind because you will start to hear sounds you have never heard before. Also, you will receive knowledge unknown to people in their worldly mind. It is like tapping into a Supreme Intelligence.

Colors will become more vibrant, and you will begin to see the world through a much clearer lens with your Christ mind. Those lenses are symbolically known as "Faith Goggles". Colors and objects that were always there in the first place will become more alive! You will begin to see them in a different light. You will begin to identify and see yourself in all living things. Shapes, patterns, and geometric figures will become more alive everywhere you look. In addition, you will also develop a feeling of being rich and prosperous, even if you only have one dollar to your name.

Through Christ consciousness you will experience a clear mind and a very pleasurable feeling that lasts. You will start to remember things instead of being absent-minded because your mind will not be so cluttered by obsessive thinking, which will lead into frustration and anxiety. Developing Christ consciousness cannot be rushed. For instance, it is just like growing a fruit tree. Symbolically, your mind is the fruit tree. In order to provide the fruit tree with a healthy growth, it must be nourished. It is the same way with your mind. It has to be nourished with the Word to ensure a healthy growth. Therefore, achieving the mind of Christ does not happen overnight because of being in the wrong mind so long. So lose the worldly mind and eat the Word of God. *Ezekiel 3:3...* It takes serious studying of the Word and application of it.

Apply the Word to all of your decisions and thinking. That is how you develop the mind of Christ. So it is absolutely okay to lose your mind, just as long as you replace it with the mind of Christ.

Authority

With Christ as your power and strength, you have the authority over all things. **_Luke 10:19... Matthew 10:1-8... Philippians 4:13... Mark 11:23..._** The Greek word for authority is "Exousia". Exousia: Power of choice, power to act, liberty to do as one pleases, jurisdiction, moral authority, and empowerment. **_Luke 9:1..._** Authority in Christ is not ever belligerent to anything or anyone. Authority in Christ: Power to have **_"anything"_** that you need or desire from the Kingdom of the Lord.

Nothing in the world should make you feel unconfident or inferior. Absolutely nothing! You should be the most confident person on Earth. You are literally royalty! **_1 Peter 2:9..._** You can command things. **_Luke 17:6..._** You have the authority/power to be at peace through anything this world can throw at you. Why do you have the authority to do that you may ask? You have the power because Jesus have the authority and power to make anything behave. You are an extension of Him. Furthermore, do not ever be timid or afraid of anything. Be bold and know that you have the authority to win, win, win!

It is just like when the police have the authority to pull someone over or to take people to jail. They also have the authority to hold up traffic. The police officer has to know the laws to enforce them. Just as the police have authority, you also have the authority to be happy, prosperous, to cast out demons, to be healed, to heal the sick, and to make the blind see. You just have to know the laws. The laws are in the Word of God.

Jesus has commissioned to you His power. He released it to you. **_Matthew 28:18-20..._** He gave you the authority to work miracles through His name. *James 5:14... Proverbs 4:20-22... Matthew 9:20-26...* Furthermore, it is not necessary to pray for what has already been released. Healing has already been released by Christ. So command it! Jesus has already shed His blood for your healing. Praise the Lord and say, "Thank you, Lord for healing me in Jesus's name. Thank you for the blood of the Lamb." Authority in Christ allows you to pray for the outcome and not the situation.

The power is God's, but He gave you the authority to release it through His Son. Demand what you need. Demand it through the blood. Speak to whatever ailment it is. Do not worry about what the situation looks like at the time. That is just the enemy trying to make the situation look hopeless and confuse you. Sometimes the pain can just be unbearable, but the pain will not last forever. Use your "authority" to enforce what you need!

Laying around feeling sorry for yourself is not the answer. You are a supernatural being that can do all things. Moreover, do not just sit there and be sick, feeling bad. You have the power right now to annihilate it. *Mark 10:51-52... John 5:1-9...* Start speaking the authority of Christ, the Healer, over your ailment, regardless of what kind of ailment it is. Start speaking healing in Jesus's name. *Isaiah 53:4-5... Matthew 8:16...* The Word of God is the blueprint on how to use your authority.

Anything that you are lacking, you have the authority to possess. Just have faith that you can do it. You can be whatever you want in life. No one can stop you, but you. Don't you know that by speaking to the mountain? That the mountain or the problem will be cast into the sea. Be unstoppable in Christ. The mountain is symbolic of any situation or problem that is in your way. Use your authority in Christ because it is your birthright to be in Perfect Peace.

Use your authority at your job. Sign up for the position that you want, even if you feel that you are not qualified. The position is yours or something better is ahead for you. Whatever dream that you have, you can achieve it. Just believe in yourself and your hard work through Christ. You can do it. "But it is written, Eye hath not seen, nor ear heard, neither have entered into the heart of man, the things which God has prepared for them that love Him" (*1 Corinthians 2:9).*

Wouldn't it be a shame to wait until you get to Heaven to see who you really were, to see all that you could have been? Wouldn't it be a shame to see all of the people that you could have healed from disease even healing yourself with authority, and also to see all of the greatness that you missed? Jesus is just waiting on you to make a move. He is just waiting for your trust and belief.

Even in the deepest and darkest pit on Earth, Jesus is right there in that pit with you. There is no way to shake Him. ***Romans 8:38-39...*** ***Hebrews 13:5-8...*** He is unshakable! Even nonbelievers are being taken care of by the Lord, but there will come a time when they will need His almighty power and authority. ***Matthew 9:35...*** There will come a time when they will have to turn to Him.

Money and material things just cannot deliver what God can. For instance, money can buy the best medicines and doctors in the world, but money cannot buy or supply healing. For example, a patient goes to the doctor for a routine checkup. During the checkup the doctor finds a deadly disease and tells the patient that they only have six months to live. The prestigious doctor said, "Just take this medicine to ease the pain. This is the best medicine money can buy. There is nothing else we can do for you." In this case, only God can save the life of this patient, not money. In this case, the doctor has no answers, but Jesus does. Money can buy a mansion, but it will take the Lord to make it a home.

If there is a nonbeliever reading this? You are loved by God no matter what. It does not matter what was done in the past. Jesus does not hold grudges. The Lamb even supplies healing for His enemies. ***Luke 22:49-51...*** Use your authority in Christ for what you need. If you need healing, you have the authority and power also to be healed. Jesus, the compassionate, will hear your cry. Just call upon Jesus's holy name right now and you will be made whole. ***Romans 10:13...*** You will be saved by calling on His name. His arms are opened wide and He welcomes you into His Kingdom.

It is the timing of His miracles that make them so invigorating! Use your "Authority" in Christ to reach for greatness and to live in the purpose for which you have been called.

Good News

This world is filled with evil and bad news, right? There is good news for you today. That is just what the devil wants you to think because if he can get people to think that the world is evil, he can get people to operate in evil ways. Actually, this world is a wonderful place like no other. NASA has been searching for another Earth or Earth-like planet extensively. So far in their conclusion, Earth is the most intricate planet out of the millions they have found. Earth is just a breathtaking planet to look at, with all of its awe and splendor. It would take an eternity to learn all of the wonders that the Earth supplies.

Planet Earth unravels new secrets and mysteries daily. The mysterious is absolutely mesmerizing! When a person ceases to be in awe at God's beautiful creations, that is when a person ceases to be fully alive. If you stare at God's creations long enough, you may soon realize that God's creations are staring right back at you.

People emulate what they see and hear. If all that they see and hear is violence, they are more likely to act violently. The good news is that the world actually has good people in it. In all reality, life is great! There is more good going on than bad, contrary to what the media and the world displays. Bad just gets all of the ratings and attention. Many miracles and philanthropists permeates throughout all of the Earth. They just do not make the evening news.

Surround yourself with positive and good people, people who benefits you. Surround yourself with people who have your best interests in mind. That means some so-called friends will just become acquaintances, but do not be dismayed. Surround yourself with good news because good news makes the bones grow bigger and stronger. Good news makes you healthy and full of vigor! "The light of the eyes rejoices the hearts of others, and good news puts fat on the bones" (**Proverbs 15:30**). That is the Word of God. **_Proverbs 4:20-22..._**

The devil makes the evening news every day and night, because people are not practicing perfect peace. Instead, they are depending on their own power and understanding. That is a losing way to live. Jesus says, "Lean not to your own understanding." **_Proverbs 3:5..._** Surround yourself with good news and laughter. Always look to the brighter side of life. This will help keep your mind free of doubts. How can you ever be depressed if you are surrounded by good?

You cannot let the world's bad news overtake or depress you. Yes, this is a filthy world for someone that is not in "Perfect Peace". This world is very dark for the ones who do not believe in God and are not trying to acquire Christ consciousness. **_John 12:36-37..._** When you are in "Perfect Peace," you have already digested the Word. You already know that only good comes to those who love the Lord. **_Romans 8:28..._** Evil and bad things will have to flee. And even if something bad does manages to happen, it will not be able to bother or hinder you in any way. You will be at an even Keel. Centered! You will have the faith to cast that problem into the sea and have a great night's sleep. **_Mark 11:23..._**

There is more good going on than evil. You just have to believe it. Do not accept bad news. Reject it! Never let bad news settle into your consciousness. For example, the news may be telling the world about how bad the economy may get. The economy may get bad, but not for you. Christian's know that their economy is in the Kingdom of God. The Kingdom of God operates on Faith. Isn't that good news? Furthermore, do your part to make the Earth full of Christ-like beings. Be a "First Class Citizen" in the mind. ("The Light of the World") One person at a time, this can be achieved.

In conclusion, do not let anyone you know wallow in bad news. Lift them up. Pick them up. Bad news makes them literally smaller. Practice daily on spreading and hearing good news around this beautiful planet.

Speaking in Tongues

There is so many myths and legends about speaking in tongues. Stop listening to what man has to say about speaking in tongues and start applying what the Word says about it. You do not have to be out in public speaking in tongues. There is nothing wrong with that either because in all actuality, speaking in tongues is between you and the Lord, and no one else. *Mark 16:17-18... 1 Corinthians 14:1-4...*

You may feel a little silly speaking in tongues at first because you are speaking in a language that is unknown to man. You do not even know what you are saying, but the enemy, the devil, will not know what you are saying, either. That is why the devil hates you, because you can talk with the Lord on a supernatural level, that even he cannot comprehend.

Speaking in tongues is just another tool to reach your true greatness. Never leave any stone unturned on your way to spiritual awareness. Use all of your weapons against the enemy! Speaking to the Lord on a supernatural level is very intriguing. You are speaking to the Holy Creator in a language that only you two understand. That is inexplicably powerful!

The day before you even think about speaking in tongues, the devil and his demons will flee! They shake at the thought of you being supernatural. Practice speaking it, just you and Christ on an intimate level. Then watch how more things will come together in your life. Also watch how you can do things that no one else can do. Speaking in tongues separates you from the rest.

You cannot let anything keep you away from your greatness. There will be times when things are not working out as planned. That is just the opposition trying to make you frustrated and stressed. It will not work! That is actually how you know that you are going in the right direction. That means you are right on the cuffs of a blessing.

The hill gets harder as you climb to the top, but you are almost there. Keep your calm. Ask the Lord to operate on things that you cannot. Ask Him to open doors that you do not even know about yet. Do this saying it through tongues and the language that you do understand. Just meditate on what you want in life. Then, speak it through tongues. It takes a little meditation and concentration. But perfect practice makes perfect. Try it! Speaking through tongues gives you a supernatural conversation with God like no other. Speaking through tongues gives a spiritual realm conversation with the Creator of all things.

Patience

Sometimes it may feel like you have been in the turbulent storm too long, but just hang on a little while longer. "They that wait upon the Lord shall renew their strength; they shall mount up and soar with wings like eagles; they shall run and not be weary; they shall walk, and not faint" (*Isaiah 40:31 KJV*).

The stress of impatience or anxiety can ruin your day completely. You cannot let anything ruin your Perfect Peace with Christ, because you have a date with destiny! Something is bound to happen when you pray. "The effectual fervent prayer of a righteous man availeth much" (*James 5:16*). Attack impatience or anxiety with a relaxed mind, knowing with full assurance that whatever you need will come to pass. According to your faith, be it unto you. Have faith! ***Matthew 9:29...***

Do not be anxious for anything. ***Philippians 4:6...*** Not trusting in the finished works of Christ will make you very uneasy. It will have you always wondering what is going to happen to you next. Impatience and anxiety makes the body and soul restless. It completely throws the psyche in disarray. Learn how to step out of anxiety and impatience. Observe your mind. Your mind is a very valuable tool for your benefit, but it is not who you are as a person. You are much more than your mind or thoughts, so do not let them control your actions.

Do not put yourself in a little box and become impatient. This world has a way of enclosing humanity within their consciences. Jesus have set humanity free and has made us supernatural. ***Galatians 5:1...***

Scientists have recently discovered that the human body can achieve some astonishing feats. Studies have found that the human body can

store more information than computers. According to www.telegraph.
com, "DNA can be used to store data more efficiently than computers.
DNA can be used to store digital information and preserve essential
knowledge for thousands of years, research has shown." In theory, a
fraction of an ounce of DNA can store more than 300,000 terabytes of
data. This means a computer cannot compare to the power you have
inside. Unlock the full potential of your body to benefit you and the
world. When a person realizes all of the potential that their body packs
on the inside, they are less likely to become impatient and follow the
world.

Impatience and anxiety is a terrible combination because it leads to
fear. Most issues people fear will never happen. Fear energy inflicts
pain to others and yourself. Fear energy spreads like a deadly contagious disease. Fear energy breeds, evolves, transforms and creates
prejudice. Impatience and anxiety will have you always over-thinking
every situation. It is never at rest and is always wondering what or
when something is going to happen. Impatience will never let you appreciate the very special gift of life. The impatient mind will always
give you glimpses of a better future when Jesus is already here with
you now.

Riches and mammon are great deceivers that steer individuals directly
into impatience. Those things need willing participants to attach themselves to them. Money and mammon need humans to love and trust
in them, and not God. What is gold without anyone to mine it? Just
another beautiful element of the Earth. Heaven is paved with gold. It
will be under our feet. The Word is accurate and precise. *__John 1:1...__* Is
gold under your feet, worth you not trusting and being patient in the
Holy Spirit?

What is fear without someone to fear it? The battle starts in the mind.
Detach yourself from a worldly, impatient mind. Drop it like a hot
plate. After you drop the worldly, impatient mind, you will soon begin
to see that the system of the world has been a trap of the devil the entire time. You may also realize that Satan has been robbing you of your

identity the entire time. The system of the world is designed to create impatience and anxiety. The devil is very wily. He persuades humans to conform to his plan without them even knowing it. For example, he entices people to design nuclear bombs, instead of focusing that brilliance into serving humanity.

The devil needs slaves that voluntarily give up their freedom and protection. That is a war tactic straight from the enemy's playbook. What good could a nuclear bomb ever accomplish? All life on this planet has value. If you cannot love, you are a murderer. *1 John 3:15...* The system of the devil fools people into thinking they are free, but they are really enslaved. The best way to defeat your enemy is by the element of surprise.

The impatient mind perpetuates all kinds of evil indifferences and pain. Money, greed, and power is a major cause of impatience and anxiety. The evil money system of the devil traps humans and forces them to destroy themselves and the planet. It forces humanity to take jobs that are very harmful to themselves and the environment. The severe need of money forces indifferences to the impatient humans upon the Earth. Help wake up the world. *Ephesians 5:14...*

Light recognizes light. Truth recognizes truth. Lead someone into spiritual awareness and out of spiritual blackness. *John 12:36-37... Ezekiel 3:18-21... James 5:19-20...* Be the spirit and not the worldly, impatient mind. The spirit loves everyone and everything. The spirit understands that impatience, anxiety, and stress lead to sick, corruptive behavior. Impatience and anxiety has a domino effect full speed toward evil and apathy.

This world's focus should be on God, the welfare of humanity, plants, animals, and the well-being of the planet instead of worthless money and items. *Jonah 2:8-9... Ecclesiastes 2:2-11...* For the lack of love and knowledge, the people will perish. *Hosea 4:6...* People are perishing because they refuse to hear. *2 Thessalonians 2:10...* They refuse to be whom they were meant to be. They are being totally unconscious to the spiritual entity that they truly are.

Most people will live their entire lives tormented by impatience, anxiety, and stress, resulting in inflicting pain to themselves, plants, wildlife, and to the world. Anxiety and impatience will have a person thinking off-the-wall preposterous things. It will start to establish fear and restlessness within them. Never let fear energy and anxiety enter into your soul. Rest in Christ. Be patient.

Suppress being in such a rush or panic for anything. Take it easy. This process is called, "doing by not doing". This means that it is necessary to work hard toward greatness, but do not worry about the outcome. Worrying about the outcome creates impatience and anxiety. All provisions have been provided. UPS... (Unlimited Provisions Supplied...) So where should fear and anxiety step in? What's going to happen in life is just going to happen. You cannot control that. But you can control your mind. Never let it control you. Nothing is ever as bad as it seems.

Continue to fight against impatience and anxiety by stepping out of your body and into your Christ mind. It will be as if turning your mind to a totally different channel, the "Christ Mind Channel," where impatience, anxiety, stress, pain, apathy, negligence, indifferences, and destroying the planet is obsolete.

If impatience starts to set in, take a few deep breaths and pray. Allocate all of those emotions to the center of your body, preferably right below the naval. You are much more alive when your body, mind, and emotions are centered. Meditate and listen to your body. Listen to your breathing and your heartbeat. Feel the blood rushing through your veins. Calm down and relax. Your body will greatly appreciate it.

So just relax and enjoy life. Be patient and do not fret about anything. _**Hebrews 10:35-36...**_ You are much more than flesh and blood. _**Romans 8:37...**_ Jesus will keep you in your time of expectancy. I know it is very difficult waiting on all of the promises that the Lord has given you. _**Romans 8:17-28...**_ It is like waiting on your birthday or Christmas every day! But in due season. You must praise the Lord in and out of season. _**Habakkuk 3:17-18...**_

Delay does not mean denied. _**Galatians 6:9...**_ God is just waiting for the perfect time to bless you and really show you He is Lord. The Lord is just cultivating and shaping your heart for His big blessings. Trust God's timing, not yours. After all, He is the one that created time. Consequently, He will be there right on time for you. Watch your mind and do not allow it to start thinking about bad things. Things such as, "What if this or that happens?" If it happens, you are going to conquer it regardless of whatever it is.

Destroy all "Reaction Loops" in your mind. Reaction loops occur when a person reacts and thinks about the same situations every day. Give your neurons something new to think about. Allow your neurons to start firing on positive thoughts and happy feelings. Furthermore, do not get mad or upset about the same situations every day. Always analyze, accept, and understand your experiences. This process will allow you to get a clear view of your emotions and thoughts so that bad reactions can be destroyed.

This world reflects the consciousness of the people living in it. Therefore, the major crisis is within the consciousness of humanity. Humanity can change the world for the better one person at a time. A person's heart has to be open to change for a change to take place. A transformation of the world does not come about by fighting or arguing with it. A transformation takes place by being the model of Christ consciousness. Humanity just have to believe it and start thinking with their hearts.

Impatience and anxiety can absolutely be defeated with love. Love energy and thoughts will drive out the impatience and anxiety upon the Earth. Living in your purpose is a great way to get rid of impatience and anxiety because your life will be solely dedicated to the Kingdom of God. Impatience, anxiety, fear, and stress is the sign of the enemy. As soon as it tries to set in, labor to rest, start speaking the promises of the Lord. Start thinking about how blessed you are right now. Whatever you need will come to pass. ***Deuteronomy 28:1-2...***

If you have activity in your limbs or if you have eyes to see, those are reasons to give praises for eternity. Give praises under any circumstance. Always claim Victory. Victory! Victory in the name of Jesus! Have patience in Christ the compassionate, and He definitely will see you through. Amen.

Notes:
Perfect Peace

_____

_____

_____

_____

_____

_____

_____

_____

_____

_____

_____

_____

_____

_____

_____

_____

_____

_____

_____

_____

_____

_____

_____

Notes:
On Your Way to Greatness

_____

_____

_____

_____

_____

_____

_____

_____

_____

_____

_____

_____

_____

_____

_____

_____

_____

_____

_____

_____

_____

_____

_____

_____

Other Books Coming Soon

* Room #515 "Only The Strong Will Survive II"

* "Shattered Dreams"

*Previous Book From Christopher Ford*

Holly Hall "Only The Strong Will Survive"

@www.outskirtspress.com/hollyhall

@www.Amazon.com

@www.BarnesandNoble.com

Chris's Dedications

Except ye eat of the flesh or drink the blood of the lamb, life is nowhere in you. **_John 6:53..._** If a person does not have Jesus inside of them. They are not spiritually alive because their spiritual food is not being eaten. If a person does not eat, they will die. Not by might, but by the Spirit of the Lord. **_Zechariah 4:6..._** Those are only a few scriptures that I meditate on daily. I, Christopher Ford, testify that the goodness and mercy of Jesus Christ of Nazareth is indescribable. There is not enough room in this book to write about all of the goodness of Jesus Christ!

The walk with Christ is an everyday ritual and not just on Saturdays or Sundays. I want to thank everyone that read or purchased **Perfect Peace**. I hope that your mind was renewed in the process. I wrote this book for a world that is hurting without the Spirit. I wrote this book for the love of everyone on this planet and to come.

God gave me the words to write because I need this book in my life too. I have felt the pains of this world and did not want any more parts of it. While writing this book I have been transformed in the mind completely. I have a supernatural mind that is continuing to grow every day. I completely lean on the promises of Christ now.

Resting in the finished works of Christ is everything. It allows me to be in "Perfect Peace" because of my trust in God. It is a labor to rest in Him. **_Hebrew 4:11..._** I pray that all of your strongholds and obsessive thinking patterns were eliminated through this book. I also pray that anyone that was sick or in pain demanded healing. Faith and trust is the currency in Heaven. Have faith my brothers and sisters... I Love You... Thanks for your support! Chris...

Chris's Acknowledgements

To Mom: Thank you, Mom, for being my greatest supporter. The Lord gave me the best mother in the whole wide world. You have always sacrificed so that I could have nice things. I remember when you took all of my friends to Astroworld for my birthday. More than once you did that, and Astroworld was not cheap! All of my friends confirmed it also. They all said that you were "The Greatest Mom in the World". You have done a lot for me and you continue to do so. It would take an eternity to thank you for everything. I love you Mom! We are on our way somewhere big!

To My Siblings: Lloyd, Lauren, and Lindsey. I love you. I know we miss Dad, but he is right here with us in Spirit. I ask for dreams of Him all the time. Dad and I still laugh together at least three times a year. Let's continue to trust in the Lord so that we can keep making Dad proud.

RIP Dad: I miss you so much Dad. I still pick up the phone to call you sometimes by mistake. Then, I realize within that quick second you are no longer here. I just wish I would have been there for you. Sometimes I feel like I was selfish with my time. I should have spent more time with you. I should have shown all of my love for you. I wish I would have hugged you more often. I am glad I got a chance to tell you that I loved you before you died. You cried Dad. I will never forget that moment. The Lord had just given me a sign that the time was near. I was really running from the inevitable.

The lessons that you taught me are still with me. I used to think you were fussing at me, but you were only trying to make me out of a man. I had some wonderful times with you. We used to laugh for hours upon hours. We used to laugh until my stomach and jaws were at their limits. There will never be another man like you. Uncle Calvin is still crying about your death. When Uncle Calvin calls me he makes me cry all over again. You just meant a lot to a bunch of people. I will continue to work hard and rest in Jesus. Thank you so much for believing in me. RIH...

To Aunt Ruby: Thank you so much Aunt Ruby. You were there for me when I needed you the most. Especially, when Grandma Gladys and Grandma Mattie passed away. You had confidence in my opinions and that meant a lot to me. Ever since I was a little boy you showered me with so much love. Thanks for being in my corner.

To Mrs. Pat: Thank you so much for being there in my Dad's time of need. You were all he talked about before his passing. Your big heart, your philanthropy, will never be forgotten. I love you...

To Theresa: There will never be another person like you upon the Earth. Maybe because we know why...lol... Seriously, without you in my life, I do not know where I would be. When I was down and out you were there for me. Whenever I called, you answered. I will never ever find another person like you. You exhibit to me a heart like Christ, a heart that loves unconditionally.

To Valerie: Wow! It is so amazing how someone can impact your life. Your compelling smile is something that I could never forget! We met for a very distinct reason. Even though you are far away, you will always be in my heart. Everything in life has a purpose and a specific meaning. It took me a while to recover from losing you. But it was that life situation that drove me to be successful. Your absence made me work tirelessly and lean on Christ the entire way. Through these years, I still think about you every single day. It is funny how someone that has so much of you is gone.

I wonder do you ever think about me. It was just something about you that totally changed me. Unfortunately, you did not get a chance to see my growth. This book *"Perfect Peace"* had been in the works for a while. It took me a long time to write it because I wrote this book on an experience basis. The turbulent experience of losing you changed my whole life. That experience taught me to stay in Christ at all times and never have a disconnection. I remember when we used to joke about if you ever needed a lung that I would surely give it to you. After all, what is a lung? When a heart would be missing. Since your absence my heart has been changed.

Just you coming through my life was truly a blessing. You taught me a tremendous amount of life lessons. Everything was not perfect, but I appreciate the flaws because I grew from them. As the years progresses, it only shows me more how special you really were. Through that lowly pain I was in, I found me. It is something about that experience that just woke me up. Through the pain birthed a worldwide Author and Motivational Speaker out of me. Now I help people worldwide to find themselves through Christ. God works in mysterious ways, don't He? I wish you and your family the best. Thank you so much for everything. To: My best friend forever... HB4ever

Special Thanks To: The Kent & Dixon family. Two wonderful families that instilled first-class values in me. Thanks for the love. I love you all!

To My Wonderful Friends: Marcus K., Shun, Leon, D'won, Niecy, Kedrin, Kay, Tee, Nah-Nah, Mongo, Lucky, U. Marentes, Fran W., R. Mayberry, M. Jones, Little James, Carl (Toon), Fife, Twin, Nate, Ken, DJ, Marcus F., Keith, Charles (Tuuti), D-Lewis, B-Lewis, Ryan, Murphy, Ashley, Big Lee, Lak, Lo, Black, Nakeisha, Cecil, Doris, Mattie, Terrence P., Tut, Alicia, A. Miller, E. Ramirez, Lawrence, Terric, Bubba Rob, Reggie, and everyone that supported me. Each one of you have contributed greatly to my success. Thanks for filling me up with confidence and supporting my dream to become a writer. I love all of you...

To Mr. McCreary: Thanks for being there for me when I needed you the most. No one has ever helped me with my projects or with writing, but you took the time out to ensure my success. Without your help I would've been lacking a great deal of expertise. I still have a long way to go, but you helped to bridge the gap. You challenged my writing and sparked a never-ending fire within me. You were always one of my favorite teachers. I loved the passion and **gravitas** that you displayed for words. Twenty years later, you are still making an extraordinary impact on my life. The Lord told me in a dream to ask you for help and I'm glad He did. Your big heart will be responsible for someone finding Perfect Peace. This book will help change lives for generations to come. I love you Mr. McCreary!

To Outskirts Press: Thank you so much for giving me the opportunity to touch the whole world. My dreams have finally manifested through Christ. He ordered my steps to turn towards the best publishing company ever! Outskirts Press allows individuals to reach their full potential in writing. This is just the beginning of real true meaningful success. Thanks, again...

Rip Adrian Branch: My man Branch, I did not even know you were sick. Your death caught me completely by surprise. I know you are looking down on me right now. That is why I am writing this to you. Thank you for having confidence in my book "**Holly Hall**". Thanks for all of your support from a distance. You always had a great uplifting soul and spirit. When I was playing semi-pro football for the "Texas Sharks," you took care of me. You took me under your wings and showed me the plays. You even stayed after practice to give me some extra pointers. "Read and Bleed," is how we did it on the football field. I can just see your smile now Branch. Your smile lets me know that everything will be all right. I love you man! RIH...

Rip Stuart O. Our friendship on Earth was very short-lived, but our spirits met and will continue to love each other for eternity. We went years without even speaking to each other at the gym, until one day you asked me about my socks. From then on we were gym buddies. I felt your pure innocent spirit. I felt love from your inviting smile. I did not even know you had passed until I took a sip of water from the fountain at the gym. Then, I saw the obituary plastered on the wall. I started to cry profusely because it was a total shock. I was actually looking for you that day. My whole work-out and my life will be dedicated to you. I hope that I make you smile from above Mr. Stuart. RIH...

Your friend forever, Chris

<u>Rip Ed Goffney:</u> It has been a very long time since I have heard your voice. You were one of the most hilarious individuals that I have ever encountered. The way that you looked at someone when they did something off-the-wall still cracks me up to this very day. I am sure that you are having a bunch of laughs up above at this world in 2018. Your smile, your laugh, always brightened up a gloomy day. Your wit was unmatched. You taught me a lot about cars and life itself. You taught me how to find laughter through any type of adversity. You probably did not know that you were inspiring me, but you meant a lot to me. RIH... Thank you so much.

<u>Rip Jesse Edwards:</u> Thank you Jesse. You were a great role model. You always treated me like I was special to you. I remember when you and my mom used to lead songs together while Charles would play the piano-organ. Those were the days... Your voice had the same tone as John P. Kee! I used to love it when you would sing like him. Those days are irreplaceable. RIH...

<u>Rip Norris:</u> I loved your passion for Jesus! You was not afraid to spread the gospel. You used to always sing with extreme vigor from the bottom of your heart. You brought the smooth sound of Al Green to the church house. I will never forget about all the great times in church you shared. You were a very special man. RIH...

<u>Rip Charles Tyrone:</u> When I was a little boy I sat in the pews at church watching you on the organ. I was just amazed on how you could move your fingers and feet so fast. I always had three favorite people that I always looked up to, and Charles Tyrone was one of them. You better believe it!

The sound of your scintillating voice used to make the whole congregation go bananas! Your passion for Christ was tremendously contagious. "If the wind do not blow and even if the sun do not shine, I will be alright. As long as I have Jesus as my power, I will be alright." I just loved it when you would sing the song "Alright" at Greater Mount Pillow. I was always eagerly anticipating and at the edge of my seat.

My absolute favorite song from you is called, "Never Alone". I was always in complete awe when you would hit that high note! No one on this Earth can hit that high note like you. That song got me through a myriad of rough times and still continues to do so. I thank God for your anointing in my life. RIH...

Special thanks to everyone worldwide, the City of Houston, Ben Milam Elementary, Willowridge H.S, and PVAMU.

CPSIA information can be obtained
at www.ICGtesting.com
Printed in the USA
BVHW081141130620
581307BV00003B/123